Singapore

Singapore

BY PATRICIA KUMMER

Enchantment of the World
Second Series

Children's Press®

A Division of Scholastic Inc.

NEW YORK   TORONTO   LONDON   AUCKLAND   SYDNEY
MEXICO CITY   NEW DELHI   HONG KONG
DANBURY, CONNECTICUT

Frontispiece: Chingay Festival, part of Singapore's Chinese New Year celebration

Consultant: Rita Smith Kipp, Rob A. Oden Jr. Professor of Anthropology, Kenyon College, Gambier, Ohio

Please note: *All statistics are as up-to-date as possible at the time of publication.*

Book production by Herman Adler Design

Library of Congress Cataloging-in-Publication Data

Kummer, Patricia K.
    Singapore / by Patricia K. Kummer
        p. cm. — (Enchantment of the world. Second series)
Includes bibliographical references and index.
    ISBN 0-516-22531-6
    1. Singapore—Juvenile literature. [1. Singapore.] I. Title. II. Series.
    DS609.K86 2003
    959.57—dc21   2003000016

CHILDREN'S PRESS and associated logos are trademarks and or registered
trademarks of Scholastic Library Publishing. SCHOLASTIC and associated logos
are trademarks and or registered trademarks of Scholastic Inc.
1 2 3 4 5 6 7 8 9 10 R 12 11 10 09 08 07 06 05 04 03

Acknowledgments

I would like to thank the staffs of the Singapore Tourism Board in Chicago and in Singapore, the Singapore Mint, and the Housing Development Board for their gracious assistance. In addition, my thanks are also extended to the staff at the Lisle Library District, my home library, for quickly putting through my numerous interlibrary loan requests and going the extra mile in obtaining the ones that were hard to find.

Contents

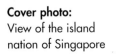

Cover photo:
View of the island
nation of Singapore

Multicultural dancers

The Merlion statue

Building a Nation

UNIFORMED SOLDIERS MARCH DOWN THE STREET; LINES of green tanks rumble along behind them; air force jets soar overhead. Is Singapore being invaded? Are Singaporeans launching an attack? No! These military units are just part of the activities as Singaporeans celebrate National Day each August 9. In odd-numbered years, a three- to four-hour parade moves down St. Andrew's Road and passes a reviewing stand in front of City Hall. In even-numbered years, the parade takes place in National Stadium.

Standing along the streets or sitting in the stadium, thousands of Singaporeans take pride in their country on each anniversary of its independence. In 1990, for Singapore's twenty-fifth anniversary as a republic, soldiers wore white uniforms and caps, and civilians wore red shirts and caps. Together, these two groups formed the design of Singapore's flag.

In 2002, about 180,000 people attended the National Day Parade (NDP) at National Stadium. Almost 2 million Singaporeans watched the parade on television. That's about half of Singapore's population. The parade's theme was "A Caring Nation." Its logo was a heart. During the parade, dancers introduced a dance performed to the NDP's theme song, "We Will Get There." The song's message is that Singaporeans have what it takes to face the future and overcome all obstacles. Other groups performed traditional songs and dances. They represented Singapore's Chinese, Malay, and Indian heritages.

Opposite: **A group of young men wave yellow flags during a celebration performance on National Day, the anniversary of Singapore's independence.**

Fireworks light up the night sky during the thirty-fifth National Day celebrations.

Because National Day is a public holiday, most Singaporeans have the day off from work and school. The parade and other National Day activities provide fun and recreation. More important, National Day brings Singaporeans together as a united people. It reminds them of how far they and their country have come in less than forty years. The government uses National Day to continue the job of nation building. The Defense Ministry is in charge of the parade. Since 1997, the Ministry of Information, Communications, and the Arts has produced a nation-building video. The title of the 2002 video was "We Can Make It." The video's message was the same as that of the 2002 parade's theme song.

The Need for a Nation

Singapore was not seeking independence in 1965. At that time, Singapore was an independent state in the Federation of Malaysia. When problems developed within the federation, Singapore was asked to leave. Suddenly, Singapore's leaders found themselves on their own. They led a tiny island nation with a few million people and no real natural resources. The leaders feared that Singapore would not survive. To prevent that from happening, Singapore's leaders started the hard job of building a nation. They formed diplomatic relations with other nations and put together a strong military. Singapore's leaders also created a new economy. Their biggest task, however, was pulling together Singapore's diverse ethnic groups and religions into a Singaporean people. They were able to do this by respecting all peoples and religions.

Singapore's leaders realized that the people are the nation's most important resource. As such, the government cares for Singaporeans through the housing, education, and health-care systems. In turn, Singaporeans work hard for their families and their nation. By the 1970s, Singapore was well on its way. Today, tiny Singapore is one of the world's richest nations.

Singapore's government stresses the value of its cultural diversity.

Shared Values and a Vision

To continue the work of nation building, Singapore's government identified five values shared by all Singaporeans. After a nationwide discussion, all ethnic groups and religions supported these shared values:

- Nation before community, and society above self
- Family as the basic unit of society
- Regard and community support for the individual
- Consensus instead of contention
- Racial and religious harmony

In January 1993, Singapore's parliament adopted the five values as the Nation's Shared Values. These values have helped Singapore thrive as a nation. The government hopes that by promoting these values Singapore will continue to prosper. By upholding these values, the government and the people also hope to retain traditional Asian ideas of morality and duty to society.

As the world entered the twenty-first century, Singapore developed Singapore 21 Vision. The main idea behind Singapore 21 Vision is "Every Singaporean matters as we build our best home, where strong families and active citizens sustain the Singapore heartbeat in our global city where there are opportunities for all." This vision places importance on Singapore's families; the arts, sciences, and sports; its excellent housing, education, and health-care systems; and Singapore's role in world trade. Most of all, Singapore 21 Vision promotes the idea of Singapore as a caring nation—one that cares for all its people.

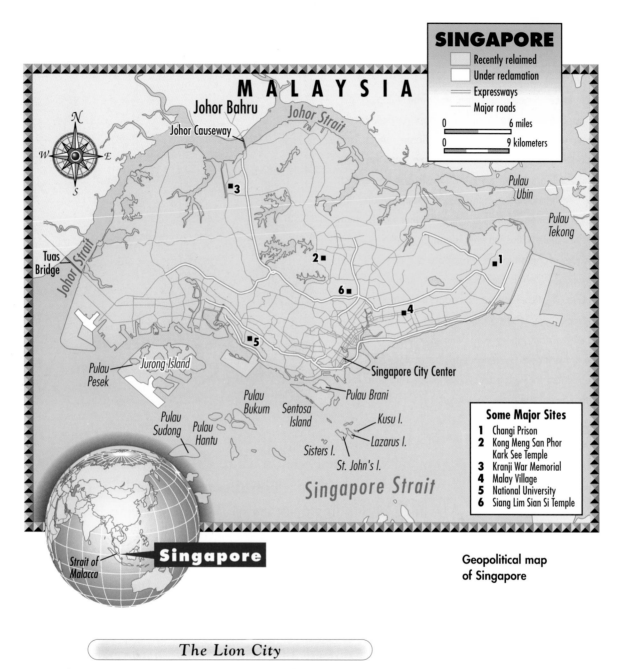

SINGAPORE

- Recently reclaimed
- Under reclamation
- — Expressways
- — Major roads

0   6 miles
0   9 kilometers

MALAYSIA

Johor Bahru
Johor Causeway
Johor Strait

Pulau Ubin
Pulau Tekong

Tuas Bridge
Johor Strait

Pulau Pesek
Jurong Island

Singapore City Center
Pulau Brani
Pulau Bukum
Sentosa Island
Kusu I.
Lazarus I.
Pulau Sudong
Pulau Hantu
Sisters I.
St. John's I.

Singapore Strait

Some Major Sites
1 Changi Prison
2 Kong Meng San Phor Kark See Temple
3 Kranji War Memorial
4 Malay Village
5 National University
6 Siang Lim Sian Si Temple

Strait of Malacca

Singapore

Geopolitical map of Singapore

The Lion City

According to one of Singapore's legends, a Sumatran prince named Sang Nila Utama, of the Sri Vijay Empire, landed on Singapore's southern shore in the early 1300s. He saw a large

The Many Identities of Singapore

The name *Singapore* refers to three things. First, Singapore means the island of Singapore. Second, the name refers to the nation of Singapore, which also includes several small islands offshore from the main island of Singapore. Third, Singapore is a city. In fact, the city includes the entire island. The city and the nation are one and the same, too. In other words, there are no other cities on the island or in the country. Because of this situation, Singapore is a city-state. The only government is the national government.

Like all cities, however, Singapore has many neighborhoods, or districts. It also has a "downtown." Downtown Singapore is sometimes called City Center. The government buildings and large office buildings are located in Singapore's City Center. This area is on both sides of the Singapore River.

animal with a red body, a white chest, and a black head. He was told that it was a lion. Because of the lion, the prince named his landing place Singa Pura. This means Lion (*Singa*) City (*Pura*) in the ancient Sanskrit language. Scientists have never found proof that lions ever lived on Singapore. Instead, they think that the prince probably saw a tiger. Nevertheless, the name *Singapore* remained. In fact, the name was also given to the entire island and to the nation.

The lion head has become the national symbol of Singapore. Singaporeans equate the lion's courageous nature with their own ability to face and overcome problems. The official national symbol is a red head and mane of a lion on a white background. The mane is separated into five parts. Each part represents one of Singapore's national ideals: democracy, equality, justice, peace, and progress. Some businesses and other organizations use the lion head to identify themselves with the nation as they work to make Singapore a better place.

The Merlion statue is another symbol of Singapore. This lion has been the official symbol for Singapore's tourism industry since 1972. Combining legend and history, the statue has the head of a lion and the tail of a fish. The lion head comes from the legend of the naming of Singapore. The fish tail honors Singapore's beginnings as a fishing village. Made of cement, the Merlion is 28 feet (8.5 meters) tall and weighs 77 tons (70 metric tons). It rests on a pedestal of glass waves. Spouting water as it overlooks Marina Bay, the Merlion greets visitors to Singapore.

The government's courtesy campaign, which began in 1979, adopted another lion as its mascot. This cute, friendly-looking cub is a cartoon character called Singa. Each year, Friend of Singa awards are given to school-age children who have done especially good deeds. Other awards are given to adults in the hotel, transportation, and retail industries for courteous service. Singapore, the Lion City, is now known not only for its courage but also for its caring and courtesy.

Half lion, half fish, the mythical Merlion is the official symbol for Singapore's tourism industry.

The Island of Singapore

SINGAPORE IS LOCATED IN SOUTHEAST ASIA, JUST SOUTH of the southern tip of the Malay Peninsula. Because Singapore is made up of islands, its boundaries are bodies of water. The narrow Johor Strait to the north separates Singapore from the country of Malaysia by less than 1 mile (1.6 kilometers). To the southeast is the Singapore Strait. Borneo, an island that is split between the nations of Indonesia and Malaysia, lies far to the east. The Strait of Malacca is to the southwest. Across the strait is Sumatra, another part of Indonesia.

With only 255 square miles (660 sq km) of land, Singapore is the smallest country in Asia. That area includes the main island of Singapore and about sixty smaller islands called islets. Its area is a little larger than that of the city of Chicago, Illinois, in the United States. Here is another way of looking at Singapore's size: The United States is about 15,000 times larger!

A really interesting point about Singapore, however, is that the island is still growing in size. About 10 percent of its current land has been reclaimed from the sea. Land reclamation is an ongoing process in Singapore. In the years ahead, Singapore's land area will continue to grow.

Opposite: **The island nation of Singapore, found off the tip of the Malay Peninsula, is the smallest country in Asia.**

Topography and Land Use

Many geographers describe Singapore's shape as a flattened diamond. In fact, its land is flat to slightly rolling. Most

A view from Bukit Timah of protected rain forest.

of Singapore is less than 50 feet (15 m) above sea level. Its highest point, Bukit Timah, is shorter than the country's tallest buildings. OUB Centre, Republic Plaza, and UOB Plaza, each at 919 feet (280 m) tall, are almost twice Bukit Timah's height. Located about in the middle of Singapore Island, Bukit Timah is part of Singapore's only rugged hilly area. Large granite deposits are under the ground there.

Along the coast in southern and western Singapore, natural erosion has cut the land into cliffs and shallow valleys. Slate is found there. The eastern part of Singapore is mainly a low plateau. Erosion there has created small hills and valleys. Loose sand and gravel are under this part of the island. A long beach stretches along the southeastern coast. Singapore's lowest point, sea level, is along this coast.

Singapore had hillier land in the early 1800s. Since then, various groups who have controlled Singapore have leveled many hills. The soil from the hills was used to fill in marshes and swamps. At one time, the reclaimed marshes were used for farmland. Now, apartment buildings, stores, and industries stand on much of that land. In fact, about 49 percent of Singapore's land is used for housing, offices, and factories.

Names of Geographical Features

Many of Singapore's geographical features have Malay names. The Malay people were the first to inhabit the island. For example, *Bukit Timah* means "tin hill." *Bukit* is the Malay word for "hill." *Pulau* means "island," and *sungei* means "river." Other places, such as Mount Faber and MacRitchie Reservoir, were named after British engineers who helped shape Singapore from 1819 to 1959. When most colonies gain independence, they change the names of geographical features named for colonizers. Since Singapore became independent, the British names have remained on geographical features, roads, and streets.

For the most part, Singapore's land is too poor for farming. About 2 percent of the land supports crops. Most of this farmland is along the northern coast. In the early 1800s, rain forest covered most of Singapore. Today, only about 4 percent of the land is rain forest. The rest of Singapore's land is made up of marshes, nature reserves, parks, beaches, and other recreational areas.

Above left: **Rain forest once covered Singapore island. Today, the rain forest has been reduced to a small area in Bukit Timah Nature Reserve.**

Above right: **The Singapore River flows beneath the towering skyscrapers of City Center's business district.**

Rivers and Reservoirs

Because Singapore is a small island, its rivers and streams are quite short. However, they flow swiftly. Most of them begin in the granite hill region of central Singapore. The longest river, Sungei Seletar, flows north into the Johor Strait. The country's most important river is the Singapore River, which flows south into the Singapore Strait. A deep harbor at the mouth of the Singapore River helped the city of Singapore grow into

MALAYSIA

Johor Strait

Kranji R.

Sungei Seletar

Pulau Tekong

Pulau Ubin

Serangoon R.

2

10

4

6

8

Johor Strait

Bukit Timah ▲

9

3

1

5

Kallang R.

Jurong R.

7

Mt. Faber ▲

Marina Bay

Singapore R.

Major Reservoirs

1 Bedok
2 Kranji
3 Lower Peirce
4 Lower Seletar
5 MacRitchie
6 Murai
7 Pandan
8 Poyan
9 Upper Peirce
10 Upper Seletar

Jurong Island

Pandan Strait

Pulau Pesek

Pulau Hantu

Pulau Bukum

Sentosa Island

Pulau Brani

Kusu I.

Lazarus I.

St. John's I.

Pulau Sudong

Sisters I.

Singapore Strait

SINGAPORE

▢ Recently relaimed
▢ Under reclamation

0 ___ 6 miles
0 ___ 9 kilometers

INDONESIA

Singapore's Geographical Features

Area: 255 square miles (660 sq km)

Greatest Distance North to South: 14 miles (23 km)

Greatest Distance East to West: 26 miles (42 km)

Coastline: 120 miles (193 km)

Distance from Equator: 85 miles (137 km)

Highest Elevation: Bukit Timah, 581 feet (177 m) above sea level

Lowest Elevation: Sea level along the coast

Longest River: Sungei Seletar, 9 miles (14.5 km)

Largest Offshore Island: Pulau Tekong, 9.72 square miles (25 sq km)

Average Humidity: 85 percent

Greatest Annual Precipitation: 135 inches (343 cm)

Lowest Average Precipitation: 58 inches (147 cm)

Hottest Recorded Temperature: 96°F (36°C)

Coldest Recorded Temperature: 70°F (21°C)

a major world trading center. Other rivers include the Jurong, the Kallang, the Kranji, and the Serangoon. The banks of most of these rivers have been reinforced with concrete. In that way, they drain better through built-up areas.

Singapore's Water Supply

Singapore is one of the few places in Southeast Asia that produces potable tap water. That means the water is safe to drink. In many other Asian cities, people must boil water before they can safely drink it. However, Singapore provides less than half of its supply of water. The rest comes from Malaysia at a low price. This water is transported through a water pipe that crosses the Johor Strait (right). Once in a while Malaysia threatens to stop piping water to Singapore. In 2000, a Malaysian army officer even suggested that Malaysia should use water as a weapon against Singapore. Since then, Singapore's government started a purification system that recycles waste water into safe drinking water. The water is called NEWater and is sold by the bottle. Eventually, NEWater will be delivered to Singaporeans as tap water. Most Singaporeans like the NEWater and say it tastes better than regular tap water. Singapore's contract with Malaysia for water expires in 2011. By then, Singapore might not have to rely so heavily on Malaysia for its drinking water.

Singapore also has fourteen reservoirs. These bodies of water were created by damming rivers and streams. The MacRitchie, the Upper Peirce, the Lower Peirce, the Upper Seletar, and the Lower Seletar reservoirs are in the center of the main island. They make up Singapore's Central Catchment Basin. This is an area where rainwater run-off drains. Water from these reservoirs contributes to Singapore's main supply of drinking water. Reservoirs in western Singapore provide water for homes and industries in that part of the island.

Singapore's Islands

About sixty smaller islands are part of the nation of Singapore. Many of them are so small that they have no real use. Some smaller islands have been combined into larger islands through land reclamation. Those islands are used for oil refining and other industries. Ferryboats carry passengers and cargo to and from Singapore's larger islands.

Singapore's three largest islands are Pulau Tekong, Pulau Ubin, and Sentosa Island. Pulau Tekong is off the northeast coast of the main island. Tekong is used mainly as a military training base. West of Tekong is Pulau Ubin. About 200 people, mainly Malay, live there. They fish and farm much as they have for hundreds of years. Their wooden homes have thatched or zinc roofs and are on short stilts.

Sentosa, the third-largest island, is also the island with the most fun. Located off the south-central point of Singapore,

Cable cars transport passengers between the main island and Sentosa Island.

Sentosa is one big amusement park. It includes a white-sand beach, Fantasy Island—Asia's largest water theme park—a musical fountain with a laser-light show, an oceanarium, and several history displays. Besides a ferry, Sentosa is connected to the main island by causeway and cable car.

Between Sentosa and the main island is Pulau Brani. Since the late 1960s, this island has been headquarters for Singapore's navy. Southeast of Sentosa lie Kusu, Lazarus, Sisters, and St. John's islands. Pulau Bukum and Pulau Hantu are southwest of Sentosa. Pulau Bukum serves as an important oil-refining and storage facility. The other southern islands have sandy beaches, clear lagoons, and coral reefs. They are used as recreational areas by Singaporeans and tourists.

Climate

Singapore is less than 100 miles (161 km) north of the equator. The country's location in Southeast Asia and its distance from the equator give Singapore an equatorial monsoon climate. That means Singaporeans live with an average daily temperature of about 80° Fahrenheit (27° Celsius).

Singapore doesn't have seasons like spring, summer, winter, and fall. Instead, seasons are marked by the amount of rain brought by the monsoon winds. From November to March, the northwest, or wet, monsoon brings strong winds and heavy rain. The average rain in that period is more than 10 inches (25 centimeters) a month. From May to September, the southwest, or dry, monsoon has lighter winds and less rain. The average monthly rainfall during the southwest monsoon is about 7 inches (18 cm). For a few days each month during the southwest monsoon period, Singapore also experiences the sumatras. These are winds of up to 37 miles (60 km) per hour. They blow over Singapore in the early morning, bringing heavy rain and a drop in temperature.

In April and October—between the monsoon periods—Singapore receives afternoon thunderstorms. Every day of the year, it rains somewhere in Singapore, giving the country an average yearly rainfall of 93 inches (236 cm). The center of Singapore receives the least rainfall. The coastal areas receive the most. Even when it's not raining, the air is heavy with moisture. This heavy air gives Singapore high humidity, with an average reading of 85 percent.

A Look at Singapore's Neighborhoods

Singapore's best-known neighborhoods are Chinatown, Little India, the Arab District, and Orchard Road. Chinatown lies on the south side of the Singapore River. It was created in 1822 as a place for Singapore's growing Chinese population to live and work. "Shophouses" (below) were built. The Chinese worked on the first floor and lived on the second floor. A few of these shops have been restored to retain the Chinese flavor in this part of Singapore. Downstairs at the Chinatown Complex, shoppers can buy everything

from fresh fruits and vegetables to computer games to a full meal. Two important temples stand in Chinatown. The Thian Hock Keng Temple, built between 1839 and 1842, is the oldest Chinese temple in Singapore. The Sri Mariamman Temple, built in 1843, is the oldest Hindu temple still in use in Singapore. It was built in Chinatown before there was a Little India. Today, part of City Center Singapore covers much of what was Chinatown. Shiny glass-and-steel skyscrapers line up along the Singapore River. Banks, the stock exchange, and other businesses have offices in these buildings.

Little India began in the late 1840s. It is far to the north of the Singapore River. Shops selling spicy curried foods are found throughout the neighborhood (pictured above). Handlooms is a sari shop with endless lengths of elaborate fabrics. Temple of 1,000 Lights, a Buddhist temple; Sri Srinivasa, a Hindu temple; and for Muslims, Abdul Gaffoor Mosque, all stand in Little India.

The Arab District, also known as *Kampong Glam*, was also created in 1822. It touches on Little India's southeast corner. This part of Singapore remains home to a closely knit Malay Muslim community. The Sultan Mosque (pictured above) with its golden dome is in the center of the district. On Arab Street, shoppers buy embroidered linens and colorful batik-printed fabrics. On Bugis Street, open-air food stands and restaurants compete with bargain watches and CDs for shoppers' attention. Stores on North Bridge Road sell clothing for Muslim weddings and traditional Malay dances.

Orchard Road is the name of a street and of a huge shopping district (right). It starts west of the Arab District. Orchard Road got its name from the nutmeg and pepper plantations that once lined the street in the 1840s. Today, Singapore's upscale shopping malls, hotels, restaurants, and movie theaters are there. This was also once a neighborhood for wealthy government officials and merchants. The Istana, official residence of the president of Singapore, is just off Orchard Road.

The Garden City

WARM TEMPERATURES AND ABUNDANT, YEAR-ROUND rainfall have helped Singaporeans create a lush, green city. In fact, because it has so many parks and gardens, Singapore is often called the Garden City. When the British ruled Singapore (1824–1959), they built public parks and set aside land for forest reserves. They also planted bamboo hedges around their homes and angsana, rain, and mahogany trees along the roads and streets. When Singapore became an independent nation in 1965, however, most of its forests were gone from overcutting. In addition, the land downtown was covered with buildings and concrete and had little greenery.

In 1967, Prime Minister Lee Kuan Yew started the Garden City program to promote the "greening" of Singapore. Four years later, he began Tree Planting Day, which became an annual event. Lee believed that providing land for parks and gardens would set Singapore apart from and above other crowded Asian cities. Now, when

Opposite: **Singapore Botanic Gardens is managed by the National Parks Board, which ensures that Singapore remains the Garden City.**

An aerial view provides a glimpse of Singapore's parks and gardens.

1 Bukit Timah Nature Reserve	**6** Japanese Gardens
2 Butterfly Park, World Insectarium, and Underwater World	**7** Jurong Bird Park
	8 Mandai Orchid Gardens
	9 Night Safari
3 Central Catchment Nature Reserve	**10** Crocodile Paradise
	11 Sungei Buloh Nature Park
4 Chinese Gardens	**12** Zoological Gardens
5 East Coast Park	

Nature Reserves, Gardens, Parks, and Zoo

Major parks and nature reserves

developers plan office buildings, housing units, and industrial plants, they must also allow areas for trees and shrubs. These oases of greenery provide shade and relief from Singapore's warm temperatures. Colorful, flowering vines cover lampposts, fences, and highway and rail overpasses. This additional greenery softens the city's landscape and makes it look cleaner.

Today, Singapore's National Parks Board manages about 4,200 acres (1,700 hectares) of parks and open spaces and 7,015 acres (2,839 ha) of forest and nature reserve lands. About 2,280 kinds of plants grow in those areas. Almost 80 percent of these plants, however, have come from other countries. When they moved to Singapore, immigrants from China, India, the Malay Peninsula, Indonesia, Great Britain, and other parts of the world carried plant seeds with them.

Singapore also has many kinds of animals. They include 350 kinds of birds, 140 kinds of reptiles, 80 kinds of mammals, 60 kinds of fish, and 110 kinds of amphibians. Several thousand kinds of insects also live in Singapore.

Famous Gardens

The world-famous Singapore Botanic Gardens is only a few miles from City Center Singapore. Rain trees, sealing-wax

palms, and oil palms line the gardens' driveways. Swans, ducks, and turtles swim in the gardens' lakes. The Chinese *penjing* are one of the displays. Penjing are miniature landscapes using water, rocks, and plants such as tiny junipers and ficus. The Herbarium has a collection of more than 600,000 kinds of dried and pressed plants. The National Orchid Garden

Visitors enjoy the flora at Singapore Botanic Gardens.

is also part of the Botanic Gardens. More than 700 kinds of orchid grow there. The garden has produced more than 2,000 orchid hybrids since 1928. Some of the hybrids are named for famous people, such as Queen Elizabeth II, Nelson Mandela, and Princess Diana.

More than 200 kinds of orchids grow in the Mandai Orchid Gardens. This garden in north-central Singapore is the island's largest orchid garden. Many of these orchids are sold and shipped throughout the world. Also on the grounds is the Water Garden, in which heliconias, hibiscus, and gingers grow.

The National Orchid Garden displays more than 700 species of orchids and is well known for its breeding program of more than 2,000 hybrids.

Singapore's National Flower

The Vanda Miss Joaquim orchid has been Singapore's national flower since 1981. In 1893, Agnes Joaquim discovered this pinkish purple-and-white variety of orchid in her garden. It is a hybrid orchid of the Vanda family. The Vanda Miss Joaquim was chosen as the national flower because of its hardiness and ability to bloom year-round. This flower's qualities reflect those of Singapore in its quest for excellence. The Vanda Miss Joaquim grows in the National Orchid Garden and in the Mandai Orchid Gardens.

In southwestern Singapore, the Chinese Gardens and the Japanese Gardens are each on an island in Jurong Lake. The two gardens combine water, rocks, plants, and traditional architecture. In the Chinese Gardens, lotuses grow in lakes, willow trees bend over streams, and walkways pass through bamboo groves. One part of the gardens has 2,000 penjing displays. The Bridge of Double Beauty connects the Chinese Gardens to the Japanese Gardens. There, small groupings of plants are set among stones and rocks.

The Chinese Gardens are modeled after those of the Chinese Sung Dynasty.

Singapore's Animals in Parks and in the Wild

Jurong Bird Park is the world's largest walk-in aviary. More than 8,000 birds from 500 species live there. They include eagles, falcons, hawks, macaws, flamingos, and cockatoos. The bird park has the world's largest collection of Southeast Asian birds. About 1,500 birds fly freely about.

Colorful parrots sit on tree branches in Jurong Bird Park.

In the wild, black-naped orioles and Javan mynahs fly along Orchard Road. Terns, egrets, and collared kingfishers live in coastal wetlands at Sungei Buloh Nature Park. Fruit bats, laced woodpeckers, and Pacific reef egrets soar above Pulau Ubin. Crested honey buzzards and Japanese sparrowhawks fly over Mount Faber Park.

Jurong Island also has a reptile park, Crocodile Paradise. Chameleons, iguanas, tortoises, anacondas, and king cobras crawl and slither around. Crocodiles up to 18 feet (5.5 m) long live at the park, too. Singapore also has two crocodile farms. The reptiles raised there become shoes and purses.

In the wild, reticulated pythons make their homes in Singapore's forests. They feed on mice and small pigs. The mangrove forests are home to pit vipers that eat lizards and frogs. Poisonous banded sea snakes swim in coastal waters. Several varieties of geckos are found in

The reticulated python makes its home in the forests of Singapore.

Pink dolphins Namtan (right) and Pann share a lagoon at Underwater World on Sentosa Island.

Singapore. They include flat-tailed, forest, and spotted-house geckos. Besides living in forests, they sometimes find their way into homes.

Sentosa Island has three animal exhibits. At Butterfly Park and World Insectarium, 2,500 butterflies from 50 species flit around. They include the plain tiger and the chocolate albatross butterflies. Tree-horn beetles, scorpions, and tarantulas creep and crawl around. Underwater World has about 2,500 Asian-Pacific marine animals from 250 species. They swim in huge acrylic tanks that curve around to form a tunnel. People walk through the tunnel to view sharks, octopuses, and pink dolphins. These colorful dolphins can also been seen near Pulau Tekong.

Seahorses can be found in the waters of Singapore.

The waters off Pulau Hantu are full of sea anemones, batfish, lionfish, and razorfish. Sea horses, sea cucumbers, and sea urchins live close to the bottom of these waters.

The Night Safari is close to Singapore's zoo. It is the world's first wildlife park that is open only at night. The animals in this park are nocturnal. They are more active at night than during the day. Visitors can watch clouded leopards and Bengal tigers. Tigers no longer roam the wild in Singapore. The last one was shot in the early 1930s.

A Visit to Singapore's National Zoo

Singapore's only zoo, the Singapore Zoological Gardens, is considered to be one of the world's best. More than 3,000 animals live in open areas similar to their homes in the wild. Trenches, stone walls, and moats separate the animals from their visitors. Visitors can get close to the orangutans, however, and even have breakfast or tea with them. About forty species of the zoo's animals are on the endangered-species list. They include the Sumatran tiger, the Malayan tapir, and the Komodo dragon.

A world's first occurred at Singapore's zoo: the birth of a polar bear in the tropics.

Today, the largest wild animals in Singapore are wild pigs. Groups of wild pigs roam Pulau Ubin. One of the smallest animals is the mousedeer. These animals have bodies the size of a mouse and deerlike heads and legs. They live in the forests.

The largest animal found on Singapore is the wild pig.

One of the world's smallest animals is the mousedeer, which lives in Singapore's forests.

Singapore's Heritage Trees

Singapore has thirty-six heritage trees. These trees are between 80 and 150 years old. The tembusu tree in the Botanic Gardens is more than one hundred years old. It is featured on the back of the Singapore $5 bill. This native Singaporean tree has become a favorite photo spot for families and wedding parties.

Singapore has two types of forests: rain forest and mangrove forest. About 11 square miles (28 sq km) of original and secondary rain forest remain on the island. Secondary forests are land where original forest growth has been cleared and new vegetation has taken over. The last of Singapore's original rain forest is in the Bukit Timah Nature Reserve. This reserve covers about 410 acres (166 ha) in the middle of Singapore. The branches of the seraya, nemusu, meranti, and keruing trees spread above the forest, forming its canopy. About eighty kinds of ferns grow closer to the ground. Feathery spleenwort and filmy ferns cling to rocks. Bird's-nest and staghorn ferns hug tree trunks. Many colorful birds make their homes in the forest's trees. They include the blue-rumped parrot, the yellow-vented flowerpecker, and the scarlet minivet. Flying lemurs glide through the sky, and macaque monkeys swing from the reserve's trees.

The Central Catchment Nature Reserve covers about 6,709 acres (2,715 ha). Much of its forestland is secondary rain forest. Yellow flame trees and wild cinnamon trees have also been planted. They add color to the thick rain forest around the reservoirs.

Mangrove forestland is even smaller than the rain forest—about 1,235 acres (500 ha). Mangroves are wetlands trees. In the early 1800s, mangrove forests lined the coast and grew along riverbanks, especially in the north and the west. Now, only a few small groups of mangroves stand along the northern coast and on Pulau Ubin. These trees are important because their root systems help prevent erosion. Their loss has allowed much erosion. One of the larger areas of mangroves is in Sungei Buloh Nature Park's Wetland Reserve on the north-western coast. This wetland reserve has 320 acres (129 ha) of mangroves. The area attracts many shore birds and water birds, as well as water snakes and monitor lizards.

Singapore's mangrove forests once thrived, but today only about 1,200 acres (487 ha) exist.

From Trading Post to Colony to Nation

WRITTEN RECORDS OF SINGAPORE'S EARLY HISTORY ARE in bits and pieces. Many of the stories mix history with myth and legend. Some of them contradict one another. Records from the A.D. 100s mention people living on the island of Singapore. An Arab record from the 1200s tells of pirate ships lying in wait for traders between the main island and smaller islands. A Chinese travel book from 1349 tells of Malay fishers and Chinese traders living on the island near the mouth of the Singapore River. A Javanese book from 1365 describes a settlement called Temasek on Singapore. Temasek meant "Sea Town."

What is known for sure is that Malays were the first people living in the settlement of Temasek during the 1200s. Most historians also agree that early Singapore was a stopping-off place for traders between India and China. A third point of agreement is that Singapore's trading wealth threatened the empires of Java and Siam (now Thailand). They attacked and destroyed the city of Singapore in the late 1300s. This caused Singapore's ruler to flee the island. A few years later he set up the Sultanate of Malacca on the west coast of the Malay Peninsula. This ruler was possibly Sultan Iskandar Shah, who is also known as Parameswara. Singapore became part of the Sultanate of Malacca but was not rebuilt.

In the early 1500s, Portuguese traders arrived and found the destroyed and abandoned city of Singapore. Some Malays

Opposite: **An early depiction of Singapore as a thriving trading post and port**

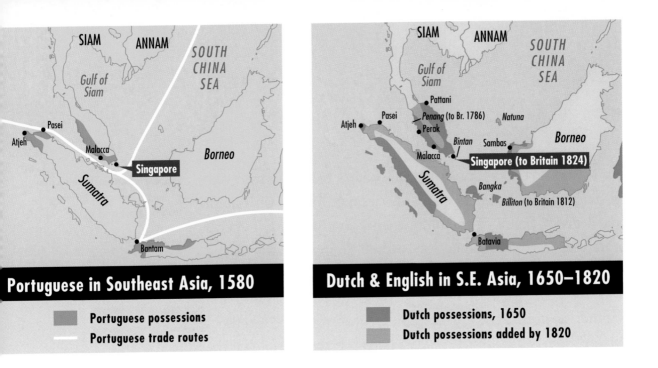

Portuguese in Southeast Asia, 1580

▪ Portuguese possessions
— Portuguese trade routes

Dutch & English in S.E. Asia, 1650–1820

▪ Dutch possessions, 1650
▪ Dutch possessions added by 1820

still lived near the mouth of the Singapore River, however. In 1511, the Portuguese conquered Malacca, which then became the center of the East Indian spice trade. In 1641, the Portuguese lost Malacca to the Dutch, who did little with it. The Dutch were more interested in their trading empire on Java. The Sultanate of Johor arose on the Malay Peninsula in the late 1600s.

In the early 1800s, squabbles developed among the sultanate's ruling family. This allowed a younger son, Abdul Rahman, to be installed as sultan rather than the oldest son, Hussein. Both men claimed to be the sultan. The Dutch backed Abdul Rahman. At this time a *temenggong*, or Malay chief, took care of day-to-to affairs of the sultanate on Singapore.

The British Arrive

Sir Thomas Stamford Raffles was looking for a spot to locate a trading post for the British East India Company. The British

Bukit Larangan, the Forbidden Hill

Today's Fort Canning Hill and Park was once the home of Temasek's Malay rulers. During the 1200s and 1300s, they built royal palaces on the hill. Archaeologists have found gold jewelry, glass beads, and pottery pieces that date back to that time. Other findings show that the gold and glass could have been made on the hill. The pottery is thought to be Chinese goods gained in trade. After the Malay rulers fled the island in the late 1300s, the remaining Malay people called this site *Bukit Larangan*, or "Forbidden Hill." The site was sacred to the Malays because they believed the ghosts of their dead kings roamed the grounds. The last five Malay kings are said to be buried there. Their graves are marked with a *keramat*, or holy shrine.

wanted a port that would rival that of the Dutch East Indies Company. They also sought to control the Strait of Malacca. In 1819, Raffles landed at the mouth of the Singapore River and struck a deal with the temenggong to establish a trading post there. Raffles also recognized Hussein as the sultan. Because of the dispute between the two sultans, and now between Great Britain and the Dutch, a treaty was worked out. In 1824, Britain acquired the entire island and all islands within 10 miles (16 km). Two years later, the three British colonies of Singapore, Malacca, and Penang were joined together as the Straits Settlements. They were on the Strait of Malacca. In 1832, Singapore became the capital of the Straits Settlements.

When Raffles landed, Singapore was a small fishing village with about one hundred Malays and thirty Chinese. Raffles saw beyond this. He chose Singapore for its deep harbor, its supply of drinking water, and its location on the trade route between the Strait of Malacca and the South China Sea. To these physical pluses, Raffles added the economic plus of free trade. That meant no taxes were placed on goods that came into or left Singapore.

A depiction of workers unloading cargo from a steamer in busy Singapore Harbor in the late 1800s.

Raffles left Singapore later in 1819 and returned in 1822. By that time, 2,839 ships had entered and left the harbor for a profit worth U.S.$8 million today. The population had increased to 10,000, with most people coming from southern China. Other immigrants included Malays, people from what is now Indonesia, Indians, Arabs, Armenians, and Western Europeans. To give order to a growing Singapore, Raffles drew up his famous town plan in 1822. He divided the city into districts for the various ethnic groups and the British. These districts remain today as Chinatown, Little India, and the Arab District, which is also sometimes called Kampong Glam. *Kampong* means "village" in Malay. The British district today is known as the Colonial Core, the Historic District, or Downtown. Raffles's plan called for neat and tidy streets. Along these streets, shophouses were not to be more than three stories high. A 5-foot (1.5-m) awning was to shelter the walkways in front of the shops. These became Singapore's famous five-foot ways.

Raffles had a home built on what is now Fort Canning Hill. This had been the site of the early Malay rulers' homes. Soon government buildings went up on the north side of the

Singapore River. Warehouses called godowns were built along the river's south side. Ships from all over the world dropped anchor in Singapore. Smaller boats called bumboats carried goods from the ships to the godowns, where they were stored until ships from other countries came to pick them up. This type of activity is called *entrepôt* trade: a country or a port acts as "middleman" for the exchange of goods. Singapore was perfect for it, and its traders and merchants became wealthy. They built bungalows and mansions beyond the ethnic districts.

Singapore's Founding Father

Born in 1781 on his father's slaving ship, Thomas Stamford Raffles went on to join the British East India Company in 1795 as a clerk. At age twenty-four, he was sent to Penang, on the Malay Peninsula. On his way, he learned the Malay language. Before arriving in Singapore, Raffles held various positions in the company.

His time in Singapore during 1819 and between October 1822 and June 1823 was less than twelve months. However, he spent the time wisely and put his stamp on the city. Raffles established Singapore as a free-trade port, forbade slavery there, and divided the town into districts. He also provided for a botanical garden, schools, and places of worship. The Botanic Gardens, Raffles Institution, and Raffles College became part of his legacy. In 1823, he left Singapore to retire in England. Three years later he died.

Two major statues of Raffles stand in the city. A bronze statue is at Empress Place, and its replica was installed at his 1819 landing spot. The luxurious Raffles Hotel was built in 1887. The shopping and office complex called Raffles City was built in the early 1990s. Raffles continues to be honored by today's Singaporeans.

Growth and Changes

From the beginning, the British and other immigrants brought changes to Singapore. By the time Singapore became the capital of the Straits Settlements in 1832, its population had increased to more than 17,000. Chinese immigrants, mostly men, from southern China made up 40 percent of the population. Many came as indentured servants and worked loading and unloading goods at the harbor. Others had farms in the interior of the island. Still others opened businesses and became wealthy merchants.

Many Indian people also came to Singapore. The British East India Company brought many clerks from India to work in the company's Singapore offices. These Indians spoke and wrote English. Indian soldiers were also brought over to keep order on the island. In addition, prisoners from India were used as laborers to build roads and buildings. Many prisoners remained in Singapore when their sentences ended. The immigrants soon outnumbered the native Malays. In fact, more Malays arrived from Malacca. Many of them were farmers who brought banana, coconut, and betel-nut plants as well as vegetable seeds to Singapore.

Changes were also made to the land. Almost immediately, land was reclaimed from the sea to extend the harbor area. Hills were cut down for a clear view of the harbor from Fort Canning Hill. That soil was also used to extend the harbor, as well as to fill in swamps. Farther inland, trees were cut down to make way for farms and plantations. New crops, such as cinnamon, clove, nutmeg, cocoa, cotton, sugarcane, and coffee, were introduced. Only nutmeg, however, did well in Singapore's climate.

When Britain ended the East India Company's control of trade in Singapore in 1834, no one else stepped in. As a result, confusion took hold, and trade dropped off. Singapore became almost as lawless as the American Wild West. Off and on between the 1840s and the 1860s, riots between various Chinese groups took place. In addition, pirates easily held up merchant ships. In 1851, Singapore came under the control of Britain's governor-general in India. He provided few rules and regulations. Singapore's traders and merchants could no longer depend on entrepôt trade. They turned to agriculture as a way to make money.

Between the 1830s and 1864, several nutmeg plantations flourished. Plantation owners and traders raised this high-priced spice and grew rich exporting it. Then a disease hit the trees and wiped out most of them by 1864. Gambier and pepper were more-successful crops. Many Chinese farmers grew them. The leaves from the gambier plant were boiled in water to extract material originally used for local medicines. In the 1830s, the gambier material was shipped to the United States, Europe, China, and Java to dye cotton and to tan leather. The waste from the gambier was used as fertilizer for pepper plants. International trade in gambier and pepper flourished until the prices dropped—first in the 1860s and again in the 1890s. By that time, much of Singapore's forests had been cut to supply the firewood needed to boil the gambier.

Prosperity As a Crown Colony

Because the governor-general in India provided little leadership, Singapore's merchants complained. They asked to come under direct British rule. In 1867, the Straits Settlements became a crown colony of Britain, Singapore received its own governor, and the city became the capital of the Crown Colony of Singapore, Malacca, and Penang.

In 1869, the Suez Canal opened in Egypt, connecting the Mediterranean Sea and the Indian Ocean. This shortened the trip from Europe to Asia. In addition, steamships made the trip even faster. The British navy used steamships to catch pirate ships. Besides carrying cargo, the steamships also brought tourists to Singapore. Singapore's port became even more attractive to traders. Entrepôt trade flourished once more.

Singaporean people did not rely again totally on entrepôt trade, however. Once again, they turned to new crops. Chinese farmers planted pineapples on the former gambier and pepper lands. In 1888, some Europeans in Singapore started canning pineapple. By 1901, pineapple was the major crop. Rubber also became an important cash crop. Henry Ridley grew Singapore's first rubber plant at the Botanic Gardens in 1889. With the coming of the automobile in the United States in the early 1900s, Singapore increased rubber production. Rubber was needed to make tires. In 1935, about 40 percent of Singapore's land was used to grow rubber plants. Rubber was also grown in British Malaya, and tin was mined there. Both products were used for automobiles made in the United States and Europe. Malaya's rubber and tin became

part of the entrepôt trade in Singapore. By the 1930s, Singapore had become one of the world's greatest ports.

Singapore's traders, merchants, farmers, and government workers lived quite comfortably. Wealthy Chinese, Indians, and Europeans lived in mansions and belonged to social clubs and sports clubs, especially cricket clubs. Asian shopkeepers, dock and warehouse workers, and their families, however, lived in cramped quarters. Diseases such as cholera, malaria, and smallpox spread quickly through them. By 1925, the death rate for poor Asians was 40 per 1,000 people. The death rate for Europeans was 14 per 1,000.

During the 1920s, many Chinese in Singapore began backing the Nationalist government in China. Other Chinese and some Malays backed the Chinese Communist Party. During the 1930s, anti-Japanese feelings developed because Japan had invaded China. These feelings continued to grow through the early 1940s.

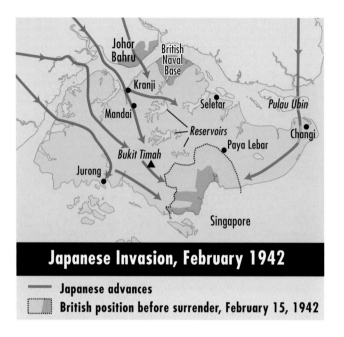

Japanese Invasion, February 1942

— Japanese advances

British position before surrender, February 15, 1942

Britain had been involved in World War I between 1914 and 1918, but because that war took place in Europe, Singapore was untouched. After the war, Japan started building up its navy. To protect Singapore, Britain built a naval base and an airfield. Heavy guns were installed to defend the port and the southern coast.

World War II broke out in Europe in 1939. Britain and its allies looked to Malaya and Singapore for tin and rubber to make war supplies. Japan also needed that rubber and tin. The war hit U.S. and British holdings in Asia and the Pacific in 1941. On December 7, Japan's air force bombed U.S. bases at Pearl Harbor, Hawaii. The next day, Japanese troops invaded Malaya and began

Defense volunteers based in Singapore prepare for the Japanese invasion.

marching down the peninsula toward Singapore. In February
1942, the Japanese crossed the Johor Causeway into
Singapore. On February 15, a British force of about 70,000
surrendered to Japan's 30,000-troop force. Asian Singaporeans
were shocked by the defeat of the British army.

Chinese civilians are herded together by Japanese soldiers after the fall of Singapore during World War II.

Singapore became the capital of Japan's southern region and was renamed *Shonan* ("Light of the South"). The Japanese imprisoned European and Australian civilians and soldiers at Changi Prison in eastern Singapore. Many Malay and Indian troops were executed when they refused to fight for Japan. About 9,000 civilians had already been killed in Japan's early February bombings. During the Japanese occupation, at least 25,000 Chinese civilian men were executed. They had been pro-China and anti-Japan before the war. Thousands more Chinese, Indian, and Malay men were used as forced laborers in other countries under Japan's control. Singapore's trade was cut back. Singaporeans suffered from food shortages. Most Chinese schools were closed. Only Malay schools and schools that taught in the Japanese language stayed open. Finally, on August 14, 1945, the war officially ended. On September 12, 1945, the Japanese in Singapore surrendered to British forces. With loud cheers, Singaporean crowds welcomed the returning British soldiers.

Toward Self-Government

After World War II, Britain reorganized its Southeast Asian colonies. In 1946, Singapore became a crown colony on its own. Malacca and Penang joined the other Malayan states as the Malayan Union. Singaporeans began to push for a voice in the government. Although a British governor controlled Singapore, six Singaporeans could be elected to the legislative council. Singapore's first election was held in 1948. By this time, Singapore had several political parties. They included the Malayan Communist Party (MCP), the Progressive Party, the Malayan Democratic Union, and the Singapore Labor Party. The MCP had support from workers and students. With this party's encouragement, workers held several strikes, and students led disruptive demonstrations.

Britain slowly gave Singapore more self-government. In 1951, a royal charter proclaimed Singapore a city with a city council. The council met in a building that was renamed City Hall.

Important World War II Sites

Changi Prison Chapel and Museum in southeastern Singapore: in memory of European military and civilians who were imprisoned during the Japanese occupation.

Kranji War Memorial in northwestern Singapore: burial site of soldiers who defended Singapore.

War Memorial Park in City Center Singapore: for all the Singaporean civilians who died during the Japanese occupation; called the "chopsticks" for its towers (above).

From Trading Post to Colony to Nation **51**

In 1954, Britain allowed Singaporeans to elect twenty-five representatives to the legislative assembly. Also in that year, a new political party was formed: the People's Action Party (PAP). Chinese, Indians, and Malays belonged to the PAP, which was led by Lee Kuan Yew. In the 1955 election, the PAP won three seats. The PAP wanted independence from Britain and union with Malaya.

In 1958, the new Constitution for the State of Singapore was signed. Singapore now had full internal self-government, and its people became citizens of Singapore. However, Britain kept control of Singapore's defense and foreign affairs. New elections were held in 1959. The PAP won forty-three of the fifty-one seats in the new legislative assembly. Lee Kuan Yew became Singapore's first prime minister. Singapore's city council was abolished.

The new government quickly set to work. To unite the people, a flag, a crest, and an anthem were created. Malay, Mandarin, Tamil (an Indian language), and English were all declared official languages. Because the Malays were the first people in Singapore, Malay became the national language. Malay children received free primary and secondary education. To improve the economy, Singaporeans and foreigners were given low tax rates to produce goods in Singapore. By hiring Singaporean workers, new companies solved the country's labor troubles and high unemployment rate. The government set up the Housing Development Board (HDB), which built 20,000 units of public housing in three years. These units, called flats, were in several groups of large apartment buildings. Millions of dollars went to build schools and improve education.

Because Singapore was so small and had no natural resources, PAP members still believed Singapore should become part of Malaya. In September 1962, Singaporeans voted to become part of a new country: the Federation of Malaysia. Malaysia included Malaya, Sarawak and North Borneo (Sabah) on the Island of Borneo, and Singapore Island. The federation took care of defense, foreign affairs, and internal security. Each state, however, was responsible for matters such as education, housing, and labor.

Singapore's time in the federation was limited. Because Muslim Malays were in the majority in the federation, Singapore's Muslim Malay minority expected special privileges. This caused racial and religious riots to break out in Singapore. Also, Malaya did not want to treat all ethnic groups equally. This bothered Singapore's leaders. Because of these and other problems, the Malaysian parliament passed a bill with a vote of 126 to 0 to separate from Singapore. No Singaporeans were in parliament that day—August 9, 1965.

Independent Singapore

When the Federation of Malaysia cast off Singapore, Lee Kuan Yew announced that Singapore was an independent republic. Lee's government started the business of nation building. Many of the strong programs it had started in 1959 were still in force, and the government worked to improve them. To attract more foreign investments, Singapore passed strict labor laws that cut down on strikes, increased working hours, and reduced holidays. However, workers received sick leave and unemployment compensation for the first time. As a result, workers produced more, and other countries began to invest in Singapore. Lee's government developed the Jurong Industrial Estate, which had 271 factories and 32,000 workers by 1971. When Britain pulled out its military forces in 1971, Singapore turned the military bases into business and industrial areas.

In the early 1970s, Singapore also built a strong army with the help of military advisers from Israel. This troubled Singapore's neighboring Muslim countries of Malaysia and Indonesia. In the 1980s, Lee established good relations with the leaders of Malaysia and Indonesia. He continued to guide the country as it steadily grew more prosperous. The rest of the world was experiencing economic ups and downs during the 1980s.

Lee and the PAP had controlled Singapore since 1959. On November 28, 1990, Lee stepped down as prime minister and turned control over to Goh Chok Tong, also of the PAP. Goh has introduced policies to open up the political system. He would like more citizen participation. In 1993, Singaporeans elected their first president, Ong Teng Cheong. Before then, the president was appointed by parliament.

As Singapore entered the twenty-first century, it had a stable government, a strong economy, and—basically—a satisfied population. Low unemployment, a low crime rate, and high literacy added to their satisfaction. The al-Qaeda terrorist attacks on the United States on September 11, 2001, however, also affected Singapore. By September 2002, Singapore's Internal Security Department investigated and arrested twenty-one men who had been trained by the al-Qaeda terrorist group. Singapore's terrorists had studied Changi Airport, the water pipeline over the Johor Causeway, and U.S. military sites on Singapore as possible targets. Because these men are Muslims, the government worked closely with the Singaporean Muslim community. The government did not want any acts of violence against Singaporean Muslims. Singapore has worked too hard to unite all its people to let terrorists pull them apart.

Singapore's Changing Status

Trading post of the British East India Company	1819
Straits Settlements of Singapore, Malacca, and Penang	1826
Crown Colony of Singapore, Malacca, and Penang	1867
Shonan under Japanese occupation	1942
Crown Colony of Singapore	1946
City of Singapore	1951
State of Singapore	1959
Federation of Malaysia (Singapore, Malaya, Sarawak, North Borneo)	1963
Republic of Singapore	1965

Limited Democracy Under a Strong Government

ON AUGUST 9, 1965, LEE KUAN YEW PROCLAIMED Singapore to be a city-state republic. A republic usually has three main characteristics. First, a president, not a king or a queen, is chief of state. Second, citizens have the right to vote. Three, citizens elect representatives who are responsible to them. This is also called a democratic republic. Both Singapore and the United States have this kind of government. To form a framework for the government, democratic republics write a constitution. Singapore's constitution was adopted on September 16, 1965. It was based on the one received from Britain in 1959. Since then, the constitution has been revised and amended several times.

With a framework of government in place, Singapore's leaders adopted official symbols for the nation. These symbols included the national flag, anthem, and pledge. Such symbols helped unite the people, rally them around the nation, and gain their support for the government.

Opposite: **Supreme Court building**

Singaporeans exhibit national pride by waving their nation's flag.

Singapore's Flag

Singapore's national flag has two wide horizontal bars of equal size. The top bar is red; the bottom one is white. The red stands for universal brotherhood and the equality of all people. The white stands for purity and virtue. In the top bar to the left are a white crescent moon and five white stars. The moon represents Singapore as a country on the rise. The five stars stand for democracy, equality, justice, peace, and progress.

Limited Rights

Before listing the parts of government and their duties and powers, Singapore's constitution lists the people's rights. They include equal treatment under the law and equal protection by the law. Other rights are freedom of speech, expression,

The National Anthem: "Onward Singapore"

Singapore's national anthem was originally composed in Malay as "Majulah Singapura" ("Onward Singapore") by Zubir Said in 1957 as a patriotic song. It was first performed officially on December 3, 1959.

When Singapore declared independence in 1965, it became the national anthem. The music was rearranged in 2000 by Phoon Yew Tie to make it more singable.

Onward Singapore
Come, fellow Singaporeans
Let us progress towards happiness together
May our noble aspiration bring
Singapore success
Come, let us unite
In a new spirit
Let our voices soar as one
Onward Singapore
Onward Singapore

Majulah Singapura
Mari kita rakyat Singapura
Sama-sama menuju bahagia
Cita-cita kita yang mulia
Berjaya Singapura
Marilah kita bersatu
Dengan semangat yang baru
Semua kita berseru
Majulah Singapura
Majulah Singapura

assembly, and religion, and the right to an education. However, the constitution also has clauses that say when the government can limit these freedoms and rights. Singapore's government has used those clauses often to limit criticism of the government and its leaders. At times, the government has not allowed certain newspapers and magazines to be published. The government owns and controls all radio and television broadcasting. Some Singaporeans have been arrested for speaking out against government policies. The government also steps in and censors or bans books, art, and theater productions. Each year, the government bans about 20 movies from theaters and the sale of about 500 videos.

Singapore's Pledge

S. Rajaratnam wrote the pledge in 1966 as a way to build a Singapore that was not divided by race, language, or religion. Singaporeans recite the pledge in school and at various national events.

Our Pledge

We, the citizens of Singapore,
pledge ourselves as one united people,
regardless of race, language, or religion,
to build a democratic society
based on justice and equality
so as to achieve happiness, prosperity,
and progress for our nation.

Singapore's Democratic Party secretary-general, Chee Soon Juan, speaks to journalists regarding two charges brought against him for making a public speech without a permit.

Human rights groups in other countries have criticized Singapore's leaders for restricting basic freedoms. Many Singaporeans are willing to live with such limitations, however. They feel that it's worth giving up some freedoms for prosperity and a low crime rate. Since the 1990s, Prime Minister Goh Chok Tong has allowed and even encouraged a freer press and fewer restrictions on the arts. Harsh criticism, however, is still not appreciated. Singapore's leaders are more concerned about building a strong nation than expanding citizens' rights.

Government Structure

Singapore's government has three branches—executive, legislative, and judicial. This is somewhat like the U.S. government. The executive branch is made up of the president, the prime minister, and the cabinet of ministers. In 1991, Singapore's constitution was amended to allow Singaporeans to directly elect the president. Before that time, presidents had been appointed by Parliament. The president must be at least forty-five years old and cannot be a member of a political party. He holds office for six years. The president can sign or veto bills passed by Parliament. Another power of the president is to appoint the prime minister and the chief justice of the Supreme Court.

The prime minister is the leader of the majority party in Parliament. With the prime minister's help, the president also appoints the ministers to the cabinet. The ministers are also members of Parliament. Each minister handles one aspect of government, such as defense, education, finance, foreign affairs, labor, health, and information and the arts. In 2002, there were fifteen ministers, two deputy prime ministers, and one senior minister. Singapore's ministers are paid well. The prime minister makes about U.S.$1.1 million a year. That's about six times more than the U.S. president is paid. The other ministers average about U.S.$827,000 a year.

Lee Hsien Loong
and Minister (Finance)

BG George
Minister (Trade & Ind

Two of Singapore's ministers attend a press conference.

The legislative branch is made up of a one-house legislature called Parliament. The ninety-four members of Parliament (MPs) serve for five years. Most are elected by the voters in their constituencies, or legislative districts. Singapore is divided into twenty-three constituencies. Nine districts elect a single MP,

Parliament building

NATIONAL GOVERNMENT OF SINGAPORE

Executive Branch

President

Prime Minister

Cabinet

Legislative Branch

One-House Parliament

Judicial Branch

Supreme Court

High Court

Court of Appeal

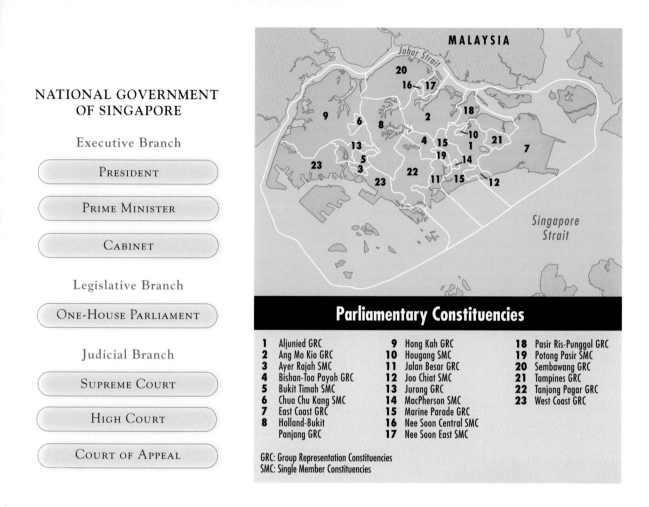

Parliamentary Constituencies

1	Aljunied GRC
2	Ang Mo Kio GRC
3	Ayer Rajah SMC
4	Bishan-Toa Payoh GRC
5	Bukit Timah SMC
6	Chua Chu Kang SMC
7	East Coast GRC
8	Holland-Bukit Panjang GRC
9	Hong Kah GRC
10	Hougang SMC
11	Jalan Besar GRC
12	Joo Chiat SMC
13	Jurong GRC
14	MacPherson SMC
15	Marine Parade GRC
16	Nee Soon Central SMC
17	Nee Soon East SMC
18	Pasir Ris-Punggol GRC
19	Potong Pasir SMC
20	Sembawang GRC
21	Tampines GRC
22	Tanjong Pagar GRC
23	West Coast GRC

GRC: Group Representation Constituencies
SMC: Single Member Constituencies

and the other fourteen districts each elect between five and seven MPs. In those districts, at least one member is from the Indian or Malay population. Nine more MPs are appointed. Like the president, they are supposed to be independents who do not belong to a political party. One MP is elected speaker of the house. The speaker sees that Parliament is run fairly. Parliament's main duty is to pass bills into laws. If the president vetoes a bill, Parliament can overturn the veto with a two-thirds vote. Parliament also approves the amounts of money that the government needs to run its programs.

Singapore's judicial branch is made up of the Supreme Court and all the subordinate courts. The Supreme Court in turn is made up of the High Court and the Court of Appeal. Singapore's president—with the prime minister's advice—appoints the chief justice of the Supreme Court and the judges on the other courts. The chief justice and the judges can hold office until they are sixty-five years old. The High Court hears all civil and criminal cases. When a person or a business is found guilty, the High Court passes down sentence. The High Court also hears

The Supreme Court building houses the judicial branch of Singapore's government.

cases that are appealed from lower courts, such as district courts. The Court of Appeal hears appeals about decisions made by the High Court. Changes made during the 1990s have speeded up the judicial process. Now the entire process for a criminal case from the High Court through the Court of Appeal takes about eighteen months. Before that, a case could take ten years.

Singapore's Government Center

Because Singapore is a city-state, there is no separate capital city. However, part of City Center Singapore is the center for the nation's government. All the government buildings are located in the Historic District, north of the Singapore River. They border the large park called the Padang. *Padang* means "field" in Malay. What is now called the Old Parliament House was built as a private home in the 1820s. It served as a courthouse and then as the Assembly House for Singapore's colonial legislature. In 1965, it became Parliament House, home to the nation's legislature. Today, the building is part of the Parliament Complex, which includes a U.S.$45 million addition. Other government buildings are the Supreme Court and City Hall. The Court of Appeal and the Appeals Board now occupy City Hall. Singapore's National Archives are a few blocks away in Fort Canning Park. Several early churches and temples and Singapore's national museums are also in the Historic District and Fort Canning Park areas.

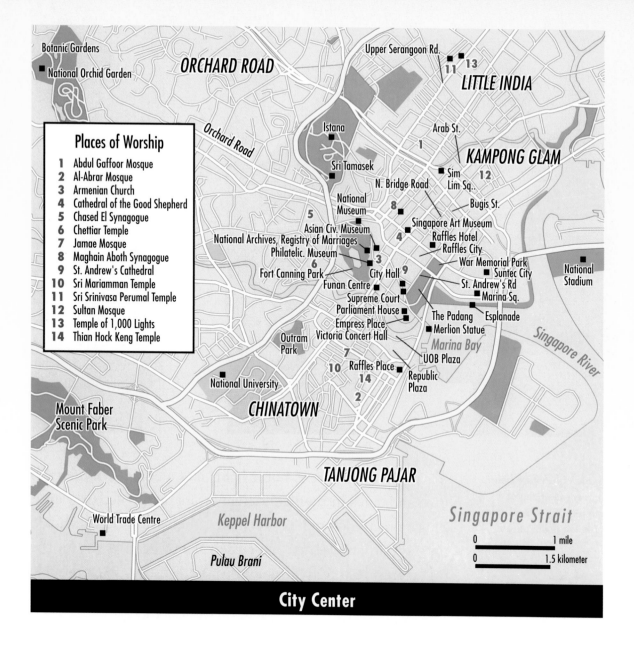

Places of Worship

1 Abdul Gaffoor Mosque
2 Al-Abrar Mosque
3 Armenian Church
4 Cathedral of the Good Shepherd
5 Chased El Synagogue
6 Chettiar Temple
7 Jamae Mosque
8 Maghain Aboth Synagogue
9 St. Andrew's Cathedral
10 Sri Mariamman Temple
11 Sri Srinivasa Perumal Temple
12 Sultan Mosque
13 Temple of 1,000 Lights
14 Thian Hock Keng Temple

City Center

Voting, Elections, and Political Parties

All citizens in Singapore who are at least twenty-one years old are eligible to vote. When they become twenty-one, their names are automatically included in the registry of voters.

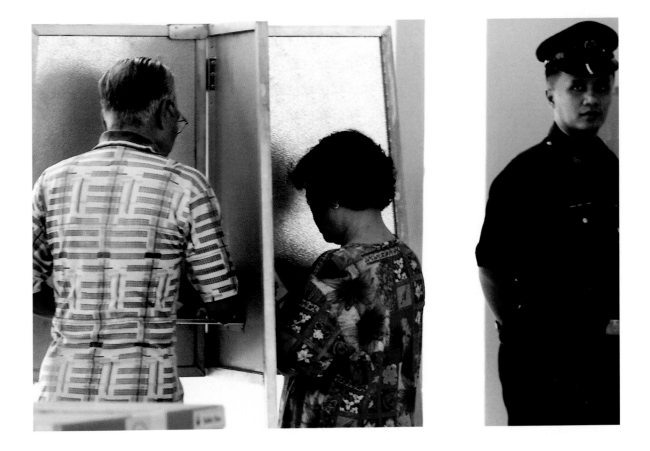

Singaporeans mark their ballots for the general election as a police officer guards the polling area.

Voting in Singapore is not a right; it is a compulsory duty. If the candidates in their constituency are unopposed, however, Singaporeans do not have to vote. Otherwise, citizens who do not vote in an election have their names removed from the registry. To restore their names to the list, they must provide proof of a good reason for having not voted. If they don't have a good reason, they must pay a fee of about U.S.$3.

In the 2001 parliamentary election, more than 2 million Singaporeans were registered to vote. About 75 percent of them voted in ten contested elections. Candidates in the other thirteen constituencies ran unopposed. They all belonged to the People's Action Party (PAP).

Singapore's Leaders

Lee Kuan Yew (above) served as Singapore's first prime minister (1959–1990). He was born in Singapore in 1923 to a Chinese family. Lee grew up speaking English, Malay, and Cantonese. He attended Raffles College in Singapore until the Japanese occupation during World War II. After the war, he went to England and studied law. Returning to Singapore in 1951, he gave legal advice to trade unions. In 1954, Lee helped found the PAP. Since 1955, he has represented the Tanjong Pagar constituency in Parliament. In 1990, he stepped down as prime minister. The new prime minister, Goh Chok Tong, then appointed Lee senior minister. He continues to be Singapore's most powerful leader. Lee's eldest son, Lee Hsien Loong, has risen through Parliament and is now a second deputy prime minister. Many Singaporeans want him to be prime minister after Goh.

Goh Chok Tong (left), Singapore's second prime minister (1990–present), was born in Singapore in 1941. Goh graduated from Raffles Institution (a high school), received a bachelor's degree in economics from Singapore University,

and earned a master's degree from Williams College in the United States. He was first elected to Singapore's Parliament in 1976 from the Marine Parade constituency. Goh held ministries in the cabinet from 1977 to 1990. Since 1992, he has also served as the PAP's secretary-general.

Singapore's president is S. R. Nathan (below). Born in Singapore in 1924, he is a Hindu from an Indian family. As a child, he learned English and Chinese. Nathan completed a degree at Singapore's University of Malaya in 1954. He first worked as a medical social worker and then was appointed to positions in the labor, foreign, and defense ministries. He has also held positions in private companies in the publishing industry. Before becoming Singapore's second elected president in 1999, Nathan served as ambassador to the United States (1990–1996) and as Singapore's ambassador-at-large (1996–1999).

Although Singapore has twenty-four political parties, the PAP has controlled the government since 1959. From 1966 through 1980, the PAP won all eighty-five elected seats in Parliament. In 1981, a seat became vacant, and a Workers' Party (WP) candidate won the special election to fill the seat.

The government makes life difficult for opposition parties. For example, the government accused a Workers' Party MP of making false statements. The MP was fined and jailed and had to give up his seat in Parliament. In 1992, an SDP candidate ran unsuccessfully against Prime Minister Goh for his seat in Parliament. A few months later, that candidate was fired from his teaching position at National University of Singapore.

Fines, Laws, and Punishment

Singaporeans sometimes jokingly call their city a "fine" city. The government fines many types of behavior. In 1992, a chewing-gum ban went into effect. Anyone selling gum is fined U.S.$1,200. With this law, the government hoped to end the sticky messes in the Mass Rapid Transit cars and in high-rise elevators. Litterers can face a first-time fine of U.S.$600. The fine doubles for repeat offenders, plus they have to put in time cleaning a public area. About the only places smoking is allowed are air-conditioned clubs and discos. The fine for smoking indoors anywhere else is up to U.S.$600. Driving offenses also bring high fines. Speeding tickets can cost up to U.S.$1,200.

Singapore's government also hands out harsh penalties. Caning with a rattan rod is one of the punishments. The British used this form of punishment during the colonial years.

A wall plaque in Singapore lists some of the prohibited activities within the city.

In 1993, an eighteen-year-old student from the United States was arrested for spray-painting several cars. He was sentenced to four months in prison, a fine of U.S.$2,230, and six strokes of the cane. Anyone convicted of making or selling certain amounts of heroin, cocaine, marijuana, or other drugs receives the death penalty. Drug use and abuse are taken very seriously. With high fines and harsh sentences, the government hopes to keep the city-state clean, safe, and healthy.

Singaporean soldiers guard the Jurong Island petrochemical facility.

Singapore's government also works to keep the city-state safe from outside attacks. All Singaporeans are involved in the country's defense. Women, children, and elderly men take part in regular emergency drills. Each year, Parliament approves about U.S.$5 billion for defense. That's about 28 percent of Singapore's total expenses. Singapore's military strength includes about 75,000 soldiers in the army, the navy, and the air force. Upon turning eighteen, every man must serve twenty-four to thirty months in the Singapore Armed Forces (SAF). These soldiers are National Servicemen (NS). Until they are forty years old, NS are reserves and spend forty days each year in military training.

To strengthen its defenses, Singapore has joined global and regional associations. Soon after declaring independence in 1965, Singapore became a member of the United Nations

(UN) and of the British Commonwealth. During the 2001–2002 session, Singapore held a temporary seat on the UN's Security Council. Singapore has contributed troops to UN peace-keeping missions in Africa, Asia, and the Middle East. Closer to home, in 1967 Singapore helped form the ten-member Association of Southeast Asian Nations (ASEAN). Brunei, Cambodia, Indonesia, Laos, Malaysia, Myanmar, the Philippines, Thailand, and Vietnam are ASEAN's other members. ASEAN works to maintain a peaceful environment in Southeast Asia. Singapore takes part in military training sessions with forces from the other ASEAN countries. SAF also trains with forces from the United States, Britain, and India. The United States has naval and air force bases in Singapore. Singapore feels that the U.S. presence adds stability and security to the region.

To demonstrate the strength of the U.S.-Singapore alliance, a U.S. destroyer docks at the naval base in Singapore.

The Miracle
Economy

When Singapore became independent in 1965, it was an undeveloped Third World country. The economy depended on entrepôt trade (a country or a port acts as "middleman" for the exchange of goods). There were few farms and factories and no natural resources. Singapore's gross domestic product (GDP) was not quite U.S.$2 billion. GDP is the total worth of goods and services produced by a country. The GDP per person was only U.S.$500. About 14 percent of Singaporean workers were unemployed. Only 9 percent of Singaporeans owned their unit in public housing.

Less than forty years later, Singapore had become one of the world's ten wealthiest nations. It had joined the ranks of developed First World countries. Although Singapore still had few farms and no natural resources, it had developed new industries. High-technology manufacturing, finance, transportation, and service industries made large contributions to the economy. In 2000, Singapore's GDP was about U.S.$110 billion, and the GDP per person was close to U.S.$26,500. Unemployment was only 3 percent. Of Singaporeans who lived in public housing, 90 percent owned their unit.

Opposite: **The busy trading floor of the Singapore International Money Exchange provides a glimpse into the successful economy of the nation.**

Workers pack ready-to-eat crepes. Food manufacturing is a growing economic trend in Singapore.

Singapore's booming economy earned the country another nickname: It is one of the Asian Tigers. South Korea and Taiwan are the other Asian Tigers. Their successful economies are also based on high-tech manufacturing, trade, and services such as finance.

The Government's Role

How did this economic miracle occur? Singapore's government has kept a firm hand on the economy. Many cabinet ministries deal with specific parts of the economy, such as finance, trade and industry, manpower, transportation, and national development. However, Singapore's government does not control individual companies. It also does not decide what or how much should be produced. Singapore's government officials and businesspeople are honest. Corruption, fraud, and bribery are not tolerated. That is why in 2001 Singapore ranked second of 161 countries in a list of the most-open economies. The United States was fifth, and Britain ranked seventh. Besides honesty and fairness, the countries were rated on wages, prices, trade policies, and property rights.

Since 1965, the government has helped Singapore's economy in three ways. First, the government opened Singapore to companies from other countries. These companies leased land and built factories. Second, when world problems have affected Singapore, the government works with industries to find new ways to keep the economy going. For example, when oil refining dropped in the mid-1980s, Singapore started electronics manufacturing. When electronics hit a slump in 2001, manufacturing shifted to medical equipment. By the end of 2002, Singapore's economy was once again on the upswing. Third, Singapore's government recognized that the people were the country's most important resource. For that reason, the government has made sure that Singaporeans receive solid educations and ongoing job training. Without that, Singapore's economy would start to decline.

Singapore's Workers

In 2001, more than 2 million Singaporeans had jobs. About 40 percent of them were women. Twenty-five percent of Singapore's workers come from other Southeast Asian countries. Many of them hold jobs as maids, baby-sitters, street cleaners, and construction workers. In addition, the government has been recruiting engineers and scientists from India, Eastern Europe, and Russia. Workers from other countries are needed because Singapore's population is so small: about 4 million. There aren't enough Singaporeans to fill the high-tech positions that keep the economy booming.

Workers' average annual earnings in 2001 were U.S.$22,000. People in financial services earned the most money. Hotel and restaurant workers earned the least. Singapore's workers and their employers contribute a certain percentage of each worker's wages to the Central Provident

Women make up almost half of Singapore's workforce.

Fund (CPF). This is a retirement and medical-insurance fund. It is similar to Social Security and Medicare in the United States. The retirement age in Singapore is sixty-two.

During the first few years of the twenty-first century, a downturn in computer-related businesses and a general downturn in the world economy caused higher unemployment. Many workers lost their jobs. In Singapore, layoffs, or job losses, are called "retrenchment." The Ministry of Manpower set up a relief plan to help retrenched workers pay their bills. It also began a center to match workers with jobs. In addition, the ministry started programs to retrain workers for new jobs. The government is also encouraging Singaporeans to start businesses.

Agriculture and Aquaculture

Less than 2 percent of Singapore's land is used for farming, and fewer than 1 percent of Singaporeans are farmers. Fruits, vegetables, orchids, and ornamental plants are the main products. The orchid farm at Orchidville produces 2 million orchids of several hundred varieties. They are sold throughout the world. About 500,000 trees and shrubs grow at the Pasir Panjang Nursery. They are transplanted to homes, parks, playgrounds, and roadsides in Singapore. Some fruits and vegetables are grown in soil on small farms. Singapore's

A very small percentage of Singapore's land is used for agriculture.

scientists at agro-technology facilities have introduced new ways to grow food crops. Some crops grow through aeroponics. Hanging on lines or from netting, the roots of these vegetables pull water from the air. Other vegetables grow in containers of water. This method is called hydroponics. Singapore now grows more of its food but still must import about 80 percent of it.

Aquaculture is fish farming. Almost ninety fish farms float in Singapore's coastal waters. The most valuable sea life are grouper, sea bass, mussels, and

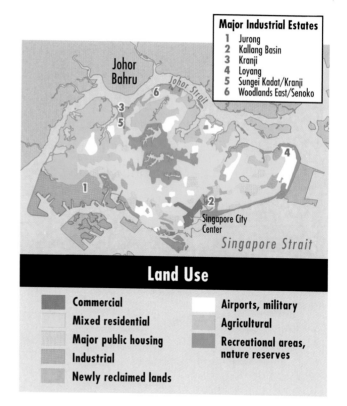

Major Industrial Estates
1 Jurong
2 Kallang Basin
3 Kranji
4 Loyang
5 Sungei Kadat/Kranji
6 Woodlands East/Senoko

Johor Bahru

Johor Strait

Singapore City Center

Singapore Strait

Land Use

- Commercial
- Mixed residential
- Major public housing
- Industrial
- Newly reclaimed lands
- Airports, military
- Agricultural
- Recreational areas, nature reserves

Fish are raised in ponds and exported around the world.

shrimp. Ornamental fish from around the world are raised in almost eighty freshwater ponds. Some of these are Southeast Asian dragonfish, koi, and South American stingrays. They are exported for use in home aquariums or ponds. Singapore is the world's leading exporter of ornamental fish.

Manufacturing

In Singapore, manufacturing takes place in special areas called industrial estates. In 1968, the government set up the Jurong Town Corporation to develop and manage these estates. In 2001, there were thirty-eight industrial estates; the largest of them are Jurong, Woodlands East, and Sungei Kadut/Kranji.

Chemical refineries on Jurong Island

The Jurong industrial estate covers much of southwestern Singapore, as well as Jurong Island. This island was formed by connecting several small islands with land reclaimed from the sea. More than seventy companies lease land on the island for their manufacturing plants.

Most of these companies, including BASF, Shell Oil, and ExxonMobil, are foreign owned. They refine oil, produce chemicals, and make plastics. Singapore is the world's third-largest oil refiner. About 2,400 other foreign-owned companies are also part of the Jurong industrial estate. Goods produced there are exported from Singapore at the Port of Jurong.

A worker makes a final inspection of circuit boards at an electronics company in Singapore.

Many other kinds of goods are also produced in Singapore. Electronics plants produce more than 50 percent of Singapore's manufactured goods. Electronics products include hard-disk drives, computer chips, ink-jet printers, and liquid-crystal display screens. For several years, half of the world's hard-disk drives were made in Singapore. The garment and leather industries make many kinds of clothing, including jeans; dresses; and crocodile shoes, boots, and purses. Once again, many of these electronics and clothing products are made for foreign-owned companies, such as Compaq, IBM, and Levi Strauss. Most of these goods are also exported. Manufactured goods that remain in Singapore include food products, beverages, and cement.

What Singapore Grows, Makes, and Mines	
Agriculture (1999)	
Vegetables and fruits	19,000 metric tons
Chicken eggs	267,000,000 eggs
Fish catch	9,500 metric tons
Manufacturing (1999)	
Electronic products	U.S.$42,084,240
Chemicals and chemical products	U.S.$8,210,460
Petroleum	U.S.$8,172,960
Mining (1994)	
Granite	U.S.$45,480,000

Service Industries

Singapore's service industries include financial and business services, transportation, communication, and trade. With its own stock exchange and many international and Singaporean banks, Singapore is Southeast Asia's financial capital. Other financial services include investment advice and insurance. Major business services in the country are real estate, legal, and accounting services. Most of Singapore's financial and business services are located in City Center. Smaller banks and business offices can be found in neighborhoods and housing estates.

Singaporeans are well connected—both within Singapore and with the rest of the world—through their communication systems. In 2002, there were sixteen radio channels and eight free television channels. About 30 percent of Singapore's

Singapore's Colorful Money

Singapore's unit of currency is the Singapore dollar (S$). The colorful designs on Singapore's paper money are based on the natural environment and Singapore's history. Singapore's first president, Yusof bin Ishak, is on the front of the newest series of bills, introduced in 1999. A different theme is on the back of each denomination. The colors and themes are: S$2, purple with an education theme; S$5, green with a Garden City theme; S$10, red with a sports theme; S$50, blue with an arts theme; S$100, orange with a youth theme. Earlier series of bills had orchids, birds, and ships on the front. Singapore's coins come in one-, five-, ten-, twenty-, and fifty-cent and one-dollar denominations. A different kind of plant is on each coin. In March 2003, U.S.$1.00 equaled S$1.75.

homes were hooked up to cable television with forty international channels, and almost 3 million Singaporeans have Internet access. About 1.5 million of them read a newspaper. They can choose from ten daily papers in four languages, including the *Straits Times*, *Business Times*, *Lianhe Zaobao* (in Chinese), *Berita Harian* (in Malay), and *Tamil Murasu* (in Tamil). Almost 50 percent of Singaporeans have telephone service. More than 70 percent, however, have cell phones, and many of those people also carry pagers.

Transportation in Singapore has been well planned. Expressways and other roads cover 1,940 miles (3,122 km). The public transportation system makes it easy to get from one end of the island to the other. The Mass Rapid

Cars drive by Singapore's Telecommunication Ltd. ground satellite station.

What Can a Singapore Dollar Buy?

Item	Cost in Singapore Dollars (S$)	Cost in U.S. Dollars
Lee jeans	S$80	$45
Nike athletic shoes	S$80–120	$45–67
Tommy Hilfiger T-shirt	S$25	$14
Coca-Cola (can)	S$0.60–1.20	$0.33–0.67
Ice cream cone (1 scoop)	S$3	$1.68
New BMW, 3 series	S$145,000	$81,274
Loaf of bread	S$1.20–2.50	$0.67–1.40
Carton of milk	S$1.20–2.50	$0.67–1.40
Gasoline, 1 liter (0.26 gallons)	S$1.10	$0.62
Music CD	S$18–25	$10–14
Paperback book	S$15	$8

Note: U.S. dollar equivalents have been rounded.

Transportation in Singapore includes well-designed highways and mass transit railways.

Container ships in Singapore await unloading in one of the world's busiest ports.

Transit System (MRT) and bus routes crisscross Singapore. The MRT has seventy-six stations and runs for 65 miles (105 km). It travels underground through part of City Center and above ground everywhere else. The fourteen stations of the Light Rapid Transit System (LRT) link the MRT to housing estates.

Getting to and from Singapore is also easy, by air, sea, or land. Changi Airport, built on reclaimed land, is rated one of the best airports in the world. Singapore Airlines, the national airline, is rated as the best airline for passenger service and comfort. It carries passengers to Singapore from airports throughout the world. Ferries carry passengers to and from the many smaller islands. Cruise ships and ocean liners dock at the World Trade Centre in southern Singapore. The country's only railroad runs from Tanjong Pajar in City Center across the Johor Causeway into Malaysia. Cars also cross into Malaysia on that causeway and over the Tuas Bridge in southwestern Singapore.

Although trade no longer leads Singapore's economy, it continues to play an important role in it. Singapore is still a free port, and it holds the title of world's busiest port in tons handled. At any time, about 1,000 ships are in the port. In 2001, Singapore's major trading partners were Malaysia, the United States, the European Union, Japan, and China. In recent years,

Singapore has strengthened its economic relationship with China. Trade with China has increased, and several Singaporean companies have branches in China. Singapore is an active member in the World Trade Organization (WTO). The government is working with the United States to gain free-trade status in U.S. ports.

Tourism

Tourism has become one of Singapore's most important service industries. More than 7 million visitors come to Singapore each year. Most of these visitors arrive from other Southeast Asian countries, Japan, and Taiwan. More and more, they are also traveling from Australia, the United States, and Europe. Visitors choose Singapore because it is safe, clean, and easy to get around in. Travelers from Australia, Britain, Canada, and the United States also like visiting Singapore because English is spoken throughout the country.

The Singapore Tourist Board does a good job of advertising the country's attractions. It has used slogans such as "Surprising Singapore" and "Live It Up in Singapore." Tourists come to shop in Singapore's boutiques and malls and to eat in its many ethnic restaurants. They also visit the ethnic neighborhoods, the zoo, the Botanic Gardens, Bukit Timah and other nature reserves, and Sentosa Island.

Tourists enjoy the sights of Chinatown.

Becoming the Singaporean People

84

For more than 200 years, Singapore's Malay, Chinese, and Indian peoples lived under British colonial rule. The British kept the main ethnic groups separated in their own neighborhoods—Chinatown, Little India, and the Arab District (Kampong Glam). When Singapore became independent, all of that changed. Singapore's new government realized that all the ethnic groups would have to work together for the new nation to succeed. Even though more than half of the people were Chinese, all groups would be treated as equals. Singapore's constitution states, "All persons are equal before the law and entitled to equal protection of the law. . . .There shall be no discrimination against citizens of Singapore on the grounds of . . . race, descent, or place of birth."

Opposite: **The government of Singapore places great emphasis on the diversity of its citizens.**

Singapore has more people per square mile than any other nation.

Population Size and Density

In 2001, 4,131,200 people lived in Singapore. About 800,000 of them were foreigners who were not citizens or permanent residents. Singapore has Southeast Asia's smallest population, but Singapore's population density is the highest in the world. There are about 16,200 Singaporeans per square mile (6,255 per sq km). During the 1960s, the government feared that the

Population of Major Housing Estates (2002 est.)	
Tampines	217,900
Jurong	205,400
Bedok	199,800
Woodlands	192,700
Hougang	165,900

population was growing too fast, so couples were encouraged to have no more than two children. By the mid-1980s, population growth had slowed to fewer than two children per family. Singapore then faced a shortage of workers. The government changed its policy and began encouraging couples to have three or four children.

Because Singapore is a city-state, the entire population lives in an urban area. Many of them live in and near City Center. Most Singaporeans live in one of twenty-three public-housing estates throughout the island. The estates are called New Towns. The New Towns have blocks of high-rise apartment buildings. The Housing Development Board (HDB) built these estates to move people out of the congested ethnic neighborhoods. In the process, shophouses and kampongs—the original villages—were torn down. Today, people from all ethnic groups live together in the estates.

Most Singaporeans live in high-rise apartment buildings.

Singapore's Many Peoples

At 77 percent, Singapore's Chinese people still make up a majority of the population. In the 1800s and early 1900s, most of their families came to Singapore from five provinces in southern China. People from each province spoke a different dialect of Chinese. Another group of Chinese people are the *Peranakans*, or Straits Chinese. They are descendants of Chinese merchants who settled in Malacca in the 1700s. The merchants married Malay women, and their children were called Peranakans. Male Peranakans are called *babas*; female Peranakans, *nyonyas*. They quickly learned to speak English and sent their children to schools and colleges in England. Today, the Peranakans make up less than 1 percent of Singapore's population, but they are among the wealthiest. They have Chinese names but observe Malay customs. In recent years, more Chinese people have come from Hong Kong, Taiwan, and the People's Republic of China. Many of them work in Singapore's high-tech industries.

Singapore's second-largest ethnic group, at 14 percent, is the Malays. Malay people were in Singapore when Thomas Stamford Raffles arrived in 1819. They are regarded as Singapore's indigenous people, similar to

Singaporean street trader of Chinese descent

Native Americans in the United States and First Nations Peoples in Canada. The Malays originally came from the areas that are now Malaysia and Indonesia. Today, many Malays are dissatisfied with life in Singapore. They tend to hold lower-level jobs, do more poorly in school, and have a higher crime rate than other ethnic groups.

Indians form Singapore's third-largest ethnic group, with 8 percent of the population. Most of them trace their family histories back to the Tamils of southern India and Sri Lanka. Other Singaporean Indians came from what are now Pakistan and Bangladesh. Today, many Indians work in banking, the law, and retail trade.

This Singaporean woman of Indian descent works in one of Singapore's fabric shops.

Singapore's fourth-largest ethnic group is called "Other." It makes up 1 percent of the population. The "Other" group includes British and other European people, North Americans, Australians, New Zealanders, Japanese, Eurasians, and Arabs. Most of these people came to Singapore recently. Many of them work in Singapore's high-tech industries. Some represent companies based in other parts of the world.

Who Lives in Singapore? (2000 Census)

Chinese	77 percent
Malays	14 percent
Indian	8 percent
Other	1 percent

Singapore's Many Languages

Singapore has four official languages: Malay, Chinese (Mandarin), Tamil, and English. Many Singaporeans speak two or more languages. They are taught at least two languages in school. They learn Malay, Chinese, or Tamil as their "mother tongue," and they also learn English. English is the language that all Singaporeans have in common. It is used in the workplace and by the government. In 1987, English became the official language of instruction in the schools. All subjects except the mother tongues are now taught in English. In this way, English helps unite all Singaporeans and aids in building the nation. Malay is the national language because the Malays are Singapore's indigenous people. The words to the national anthem are in Malay.

A street sign in English and Chinese

Although there is one written Chinese language, there are many spoken dialects. The main dialects in Singapore are

Using Singapore's National Language

Malay, the national language of Singapore, is fairly easy to learn. Because there are no verb tenses, the same word expresses present and future. For the past tense, *suda* is added to the word. Also, there are no articles, such as *a*, *an*, or *the*. Malay nouns do not have gender. Pronouncing Malay is quite easy, too. The accent is on the next to the last syllable of each word. Most letters sound as they are written. Cs are pronounced *ch*, as in *chant*. When speaking Malay, Singaporeans roll their *r*s.

a = *ah* in father
e = *eh* in bed
i = *ee* in meet
o = *aw* in all
u = *u* in foot
c = *ch* in chant

Hokkien, Teochew, Cantonese, Hakka, and Hainanese. The early Chinese immigrants brought these dialects with them. In addition, the Peranakans speak a Malay dialect that also uses words from the Hokkien dialect. In 1979, Prime Minister Lee Kuan Yew started a campaign called Speak Mandarin. Mandarin is the official spoken language in China. Speak Mandarin is an ongoing program. One aim of Speak Mandarin is to make it easier for Singapore's Chinese people to understand one another. Also, if Singaporeans learn Mandarin, they will have an easier time doing business in China.

Tamil is another official language. About 60 percent of the Indians in Singapore speak Tamil. Other languages from India spoken by Singaporean Indians are Bengali, Hindi, Malayalam, Punjabi, and Telegu. Many Tamil-speaking children are also learning to speak Mandarin, as well as the required English. Many Indians also speak Malay.

Another language has developed in Singapore. It is called *Singlish*, for *Singapore English*. Singlish is a combination of standard English with Chinese, Malay, and Tamil words.

Common Words and Phrases in Singapore's Four Languages

English	Malay	Chinese	Tamil
Hello/How are you?	Apa khabar?	Ni hao?	Vanakkam?
Good-bye	Selamat jalan	Zai-jia	Poyittu varukiren
Excuse me.	Maafkan saya.	Duibuqi.	Mannikkavum.
Please	Sila	Qing	Tayavu seytu
Thank you.	Terima kasih.	Xie xie.	Nanri.
Yes	Ya	Dui	Am
No	Tidak	Bu	Illai

Sentences frequently end with the word *lah*, which is Malay for "you know." Some examples of Singlish are "I go there now"; "She never come"; "Aiyah, you!" for "Why are you so late?"; "Can lah" instead of "I can do it." Singaporeans use this "language" with friends and neighbors even though they use standard English at work or in school. To some, Singlish is just bad English. In fact, Prime Minister Goh Chok Tong started a

Names in Singapore

Personal names, family names, and the order in which they are used are different for each of Singapore's ethnic groups. Chinese names usually have three parts. The family name comes first, then the two parts of the personal name. For example, Prime Minister Lee Kuan Yew's family name is Lee. Some Chinese use Western personal names. Those names then come first. For example, when Lee was a young man, he went by the Western name of Harry, so he was called Harry Lee.

Malay Singaporeans do not have family names. Malays have a personal name that is followed by their father's name. The two names are connected by *bin* for "son of" or *binti* for "daughter of." For example, President Yusof bin Ishak was Yusof son of Ishak.

Indian Singaporeans do not have family names either. They use the initial or initials of their father's name in front of their personal name. For example, President S. R. Nathan has the initials of his father's names, Sellapan Rama. Some Indian Singaporeans have started using family names. They might choose their own name or their father's name to pass down to their children and grandchildren.

campaign in 2000 to decrease the use of Singlish. This campaign is the Speak Good English Movement.

Housing, Education, and Health

About 85 percent of Singaporeans live in public-housing estates in New Towns. About 90 percent of these people own their own apartment. Singaporeans call apartments "flats." The flats range in size from one room to five rooms. Singaporeans can take money from their CPF accounts to help pay for their flat. Other Singaporeans live in private housing. They own or rent flats, condominiums, or single-family homes. Some Malays still live in kampongs on Pulau Ubi. Their kampongs on the main island were torn down to make room for housing estates.

Education was not compulsory in Singapore until 2003. Even before that year, however, most Singaporeans received solid educations. Proof of that was Singapore's high literacy

Singapore's children were not required to attend school until 2003.

rate—93 percent in 2001. Most of Singapore's schools are public, government-supported schools. Students are guaranteed ten years of public education. Children ages six to eleven attend primary school. Children in secondary school are twelve to fifteen. A typical eleven-year-old would study English, the mother tongue, math, humanities, science, civics, home economics or design and technology, art, music, and physical education. Children from all ethnic groups attend classes together in the public schools.

After secondary school, students can follow one of two two-year tracks. One track involves an apprenticeship or vocational education that leads to a job. The other track takes them to a junior college or a polytechnic school that prepares students for the university.

There are also private schools that educate the children of people from other countries, such as the Singapore American School, the Japanese School, and the German School. Other private schools are run by Islamic groups and by the Catholic Church.

Besides having good housing and education programs, Singapore promotes good health. Singaporeans are the healthiest people in Southeast Asia. They have a safe water supply; a clean environment; some of the best hospitals; and many doctors, nurses, and dentists. As a result, the infant death rate in Singapore is low. Only 2.2 babies in 1,000 die. The rate in the United States is higher, 6.7 babies in 1,000. Singaporeans can also expect to live to about age seventy-eight. The average life expectancy in the United States is about seventy-seven.

Respecting Many Religions

ALL THE MAJOR RELIGIONS OF THE WORLD ARE REPRE-
sented in Singapore. They are Buddhism, Christianity,
Hinduism, Islam, and Judaism. Other belief systems include
Taoism, Sikhism, and Jainism. Singapore's many ethnic groups
brought these religions to
Singapore. In the 1800s, they
built Buddhist and Hindu temples, Christian churches, and
Islamic mosques that still stand.

Most Singaporeans continue
to hold the beliefs of their immi-
grant ancestors. Buddhism and
Taoism are the main religions of
the Chinese community. Almost
all Malays and some northern
Indians observe Islam. Most
Indians are Hindus, although
Indians from Punjab are Sikhs.
Europeans, Eurasians, and some
younger Chinese make up
Singapore's Christian community.

Because Singapore has so
many faiths, religious tolerance
has been part of life since the
1800s. Singapore has no one official

Opposite: **A Chinese worshiper lights incense in a Buddhist temple.**

Women at a Hindu evening prayer service

Religions of Singapore

Buddhism	42.5%
Islam	14.9%
Christianity	14.6%
Taoism	8.5%
Hinduism	4.0%
Other (Judaism, Sikhism, Jainism)	0.6%
No religion	14.9%

religion, and there is separation of church and state. Singapore's constitution guarantees religious freedom. It states, "Every person has the right to profess and practice his religion and to propagate it. . . . Every religious group has the right to manage its own religious affairs."

Beliefs and Practices

The prophet Muhammad founded Islam in the A.D. 600s in what is now Saudi Arabia. Arab and Indian traders brought Islam to Southeast Asia in the 1100s. Malay people throughout the region became Muslims, followers of Islam. Singapore's Muslims observe the Five Pillars of Islam. First, they believe in one God, called Allah, with Muhammad as his prophet. Second, they pray five times a day—at sunrise, mid-morning,

Friday prayers at Sultan Mosque

mid-afternoon, sunset, and night. They are reminded to pray by recorded broadcasts. Third, they make gifts to charity. Fourth, they observe a daytime fast during the month of Ramadan. Fifth, if possible, they make a pilgrimage to Mecca in Saudi Arabia, the city of Muhammad's birth. Most of Singapore's Muslims do not eat pork. Friday is the Islamic Sabbath. On Fridays from 11:30 in the morning to 2:30 in the afternoon, Muslims go to their mosque to pray. Men and women do not pray together, however. Many Muslims send their children to Islamic schools. There they study Islam and the Arabic language.

This mural hangs in a Hindu temple and depicts the many gods and goddesses worshiped.

Hinduism began in India about 3,000 years ago. Hindus believe in a universal spirit called Brahman who has three forms. They are Brahma, who creates life; Vishnu, who preserves life; and Shiva, who destroys life. There are also many other colorful Hindu gods and goddesses, such as elephant-headed Ganesha and red-tongued Kali. The main Hindu belief is reincarnation. Through reincarnation, people are reborn again and again. The form of life to which they are reborn depends on their behavior in their previous life, or *karma*. In Singapore, Hindus visit their temple once a week. Priests perform ceremonies in the temples. Because there is a shortage of Hindu priests in Singapore, the temples pay for priests to come from India.

Sikhism is another religion from India. Although few Singaporeans observe Sikhism, those who do are very visible. The men do not cut their hair but wear it wrapped up in a turban.

Sikhism combines ideas from Islam and Hinduism. Sikhs believe in one God and in reincarnation. They also believe in a chosen race of soldier-saints. Many Sikhs were among the soldiers that the British brought from India to Singapore. Their descendants follow Sikhism today.

The Chinese brought Buddhism, Taoism, and traditional Chinese religions. In the traditional religions, Chinese people pray to gods of nature for help. They also honor their ancestors by making offerings at shrines and temples. Buddhism began in India in the 500s B.C. and

Men who follow Sikhism do not cut their hair but wrap it in a turban.

spread to eastern Asia, including China. Buddhists, like Hindus, believe in reincarnation based on how a person lived the previous life. Buddhists, however, believe that people can end the reincarnation cycle and achieve *nirvana*, or enlightenment. Nirvana comes when a person eliminates all desire. Today, Singapore's Buddhists promote their religion by handing out pamphlets and doing charity work.

Chinese Singaporeans pray and make offerings at shrines and temples.

Confucianism in Singapore

Confucius (551–479 B.C.) was a Chinese teacher and philosopher (pictured below). Until the early 1900s, his ideas were the state philosophy of China. Confucius's philosophy included loyalty to rulers and the government, respect for elders, obedience to parents, give-and-take between friends, kindness toward strangers, and hard work. Prime Minister Lee Kuan Yew began promoting these ideas to Singaporeans. This was an effort to retain Singapore's Asian heritage. By the 1990s, Singaporeans accepted these ideas as the Nation's Shared Values.

Taoism also came from China. This belief is traced back to about the 500s B.C. and the philosopher Laozi. *Tao*, which means "the way," is more a philosophy of life than a religion. The most important idea in Taoism is that of *yin* (female forces) and *yang* (male forces). To have balance and harmony in life and in the world, yin and yang must be in balance. Illness and war occur because yin and yang are not balanced. Most members of Singapore's Chinese community combine the beliefs of Buddhism and the ideas of Taoism.

The British introduced Christianity to Singapore in the early 1800s. They belonged to the Anglican Church, the Protestant church known as the Church of England. Catholic missionaries also came to Singapore and set up churches and schools. Today, Catholics and many Protestant groups make up Singapore's Christian community. Although they have different practices, they all believe that Jesus Christ was the son of God and that he died on a cross to redeem the sins of all people. Christianity is Singapore's fastest-growing religion. Many English-educated Chinese have become Anglican or Catholic Christians. Protestant fundamentalist and evangelical churches have also gained many converts.

Judaism arrived in Singapore in about 1840, when Jewish merchants set up businesses there. They follow the laws set down in the Old Testament. Jews believe in the same God that Christians do. However, they do not believe that Christ was the Redeemer. Today, there are only a few thousand Jews in Singapore. Saturday is the Sabbath for Jews. On that day, they worship in two synagogues, Maghain Aboth and Chased El.

A man at Thaipusam carries the *kavadi*.

Religious Holidays

Because Singapore has so many religions, Singaporeans celebrate many religious holidays and festivals. Among the ten national holidays, all of Singapore's major religions are represented. Thaipusam and Deepavali are Hindu festivals. Thaipusam is a festival of purification. Hindu worshipers carry a *kavadi*, or gift, to the god Murugan. The kavadi is protected by a metal frame that is attached to a worshiper's body with long skewers. Worshipers also pierce their tongues and cheeks with small silver spears. They walk 2 miles (3.2 km) between two temples carrying the kavadi. Hindus celebrate Deepavali, the

and other luxury goods. The ghosts can then use these goods in the afterlife and not have to come back to earth.

Temples, Churches, and Mosques

Followers of each of Singapore's major religions have built beautiful places of worship. Chinese shrines and Buddhist temples are built with wood. Their green-tile roofs curve up at the edges. Thian Hock Keng is Singapore's oldest Chinese

Thian Hock Keng, the oldest Chinese temple in Singapore

Statue of Buddha in the
Temple of 1,000 Lights

temple. Hokkien sailors built it between 1839 and 1842 as a place to thank the sea goddess Ma Zhu Po for a safe trip back to Singapore. The temple has been added onto over the years and received a major restoration in 2000.

Singapore has several Buddhist temples. Siong Lim San Si Temple is Singapore's largest Buddhist temple. It was built between 1868 and 1908. Other Buddhist temples include the Temple of 1,000 Lights. Colored electric lights shine on a

Seventy-two gods and goddesses adorn Singapore's oldest Hindu temple, Sri Mariamman.

50-foot- (15-m-) high statue of a seated Buddha. Built in 1981, the Kong Meng San Phor Kark See Temple is one of Singapore's newest Buddhist temples. It is known for its crematorium and the space that can hold up to 300,000 urns of cremated remains.

Singapore's Hindus built large, colorful temples. Each temple is devoted to the worship of a Hindu god or goddess. All Hindu temples have a large tower, called a *gopuram*. Worshipers enter the main part of the temple through a door in the tower. The Sri Mariamman Temple is the oldest Hindu temple in Singapore. It is named for the goddess who cures epidemic diseases. Its gopuram has colorful statues of seventy-two Hindu gods and goddesses. Naraina Pillai, the Indian owner of a construction business, had the temple built with wood in 1827. He used Indian convicts to build it. The temple was rebuilt with brick in 1843. Sri Srinivasa Perumal Temple is devoted to the god Vishnu. This is the starting point for the Thaipusam festival that ends at Chettiar Temple. *Chettiars*, Indian moneylenders, built this temple to honor the god Murugan.

Muslims in Singapore have built more than eighty mosques. The main features of mosques are large golden domes and four narrow towers called minarets. All mosques are built so that worshipers face the Muslim holy city of Mecca. The largest mosque is the Sultan Mosque. It was built in the Arab District in 1826 with money from the East India Company, paid in return for gaining ownership of Singapore. It was named for the Malay sultan who ruled Singapore at that

time. The current building was constructed in 1928. More than 5,000 people can worship in its main prayer hall.

The most famous Christian churches in Singapore are the Church of Saint Gregory the Illuminator, Saint Andrew's Cathedral, and the Cathedral of the Good Shepherd. Saint Gregory was built in 1835 by Singapore's small Armenian community. It is the oldest Christian church on the island. Saint Andrew's is the main Anglican church in Singapore. The current building was completed in 1861. Its white walls were made with a special plaster, a mixture of egg whites, crushed shells, lime, sugar, coconut husks, and water. The Cathedral of the Good Shepherd is the main Catholic church in Singapore. It was completed in 1847. One feature of this church is its eight-sided steeple.

Opposite: **The Sultan Mosque, the largest mosque in Singapore**

Saint Andrew's Cathedral

A Modern Culture with Traditions

SINGAPORE HAS A RICH CULTURE BASED ON ITS MALAY, Chinese, Indian, and Western heritages. Singaporeans practice their traditional music and dance. They also observe special marriage and funeral customs. Many Singaporeans enjoy modern literature, music, and art, too. Playing sports is another way Singaporeans interact with one another. Singapore's government supports the arts and sports through two ministries.

The Ministry of Information, Communication, and the Arts promotes Singapore's multicultural heritage and fosters modern developments. The Ministry of Community Development and Sports works to build a united society of "responsible individuals, strong and stable families . . . and a sporting people." The People's Association and the Singapore Sports Council are under this ministry.

Some people have criticized the arts in Singapore, saying that they haven't been progressive. They blame Singapore's government for not allowing artists full free expression. As a result, many artists and writers have left the country to work in freer environments. This problem is slowly being corrected. In the 1990s, Prime Minister Goh Chok Tong started promoting programs that would encourage more artistic expression and bring Singaporean artists back home.

Opposite: **Chinese opera performer**

A Modern Culture with Traditions **111**

Marriage Customs

Most Singaporeans have two wedding ceremonies. The first one is a civil ceremony at the Registry of Marriages. Later, the couple has a wedding celebration with their families. Each of Singapore's ethnic groups has its own wedding customs. In most Chinese weddings in Singapore, the bride wears a white gown and veil, and the groom wears a black tuxedo (pictured right). They perform a tea ceremony with their family and then receive gifts. From there, they attend a multicourse dinner for family, relatives, and friends.

A Malay Muslim wedding could extend over a weekend. The bride and the groom wear elaborate costumes in matching material. They walk in a procession outdoors to a raised platform where they sit (pictured below) and are treated as a king and a queen by their guests. Hindu weddings are also colorful and can last several hours. The bride wears a red sari, and the groom wears a white jacket and pants.

Traditional Arts

Chinese street opera, *wayang*, remains popular in Singapore. Performances take place on stages outdoors, especially during the Hungry Ghosts festival. The operas are based on Chinese folk tales and legends. The actors wear boldly colored costumes and makeup that tell the characters' age and social status. Their singing is accompanied by loud cymbals, drums, and gongs. Stories of the Peranakans are brought to life in plays in small theaters.

Wayang, or Chinese street opera, performers

In a special area called Malay Village, Malays perform traditional dances. Some Malay dances tell a story. Others are enjoyed just for the dancing. Dancers are usually accompanied by *gamelan* players. Gamelans are chimes and gongs. Other traditional Malay instruments include the *kertok*, a single-bar xylophone, and the *tali*, a three-stringed fiddle. *Hangsawan*, Malay opera, tells its stories in a dramatic fashion much like Chinese opera.

Bharathanatyam is a traditional dance form from southern India. Its intricate hand and finger movements must be done just right to tell a story. Singapore's Indians also use traditional musical instruments. One of them is the *pungi*, which makes a sound similar to that of a bagpipe.

Singapore's writers have become bolder in recent years. Catherine Lim has published several novels and short stories, such as *Little Ironies* and *O Singapore! Stories in Celebration*. They take a close look at Singapore's progress and question whether it has brought unity and success. Gopal Baratham's novels look at the less pleasant parts of life in Singapore. His most famous novel is *A Candle or the Sun*. Some Singaporeans have written political humor. *Kampong Boy*, by Lat (Mohamad Nor Khalid), is a cartoon book about Malay life that also pokes fun at political leaders. George Nonis wrote *Hello Chok Tong, Goodby Kuan Yew*. This is a comic book about the two prime ministers.

Several artists have become well known in Singapore, too. Most of them studied at the Nanyang Academy of Fine Arts. Foo Chee San is known for his serene landscapes, such as *Spring Woods*, *Source*, and *Tropical Fruit*. S. Chandrasekaran bases his works on Hindu-Buddhist thought. Mohamed Abdul Kadir's *Sandiwara*, which means "Play" in Malay, is a multilayered painting of chairs and tables in a café. Amanda Heng's works are related to women's topics. *She and Her Dishcover* comments on how women's work at home is considered secondary to men's work outside the home.

Modern music in Singapore ranges from classical to popular. The Singapore Symphony Orchestra performs Western classical music at Victoria Concert Hall. Sometimes music from Asian composers is also played. Some Singaporean rock bands are making news, too. They have names such as

Georgette Chen: Singapore's Most Influential Artist

Georgette Chen (1906–1993) was born in China, but she grew up in Paris, France. She studied art in Paris and was influenced by French impressionism. In 1930, she met and married Eugene Chen, a diplomat for China in Paris. They spent long periods of time in China, where she learned Chinese techniques and ideas for painting.

After her husband died, Chen moved to Singapore, settling there in 1953. From 1954 to 1981, she taught art at the Nanyang Academy of Fine Arts. She was named a Pioneer Artist of Singapore and was awarded the Cultural Medallion in 1982 for her outstanding achievements and contributions to art.

Chen is best known for her still lifes of baskets with tropical fruits and vegetables. She also did several portraits of her husband and a self-portrait. *Singapore Waterfront*, one of her landscapes/seascapes, depicts shophouses and bumboats in 1958.

Stomping Ground, Flying Pills, and the Lilac Saints. Singapore even has a few pop stars, such as Aaron Kook and Karen Mk. They put on elaborate stage shows similar to U.S. rock concerts.

Singapore has also returned to making movies. For many years, Singaporeans preferred to watch movies made in the United States. *Forever Fever* is one of Singapore's most famous films. It has been shown in many other countries. Its story is similar to that of the U.S. film *Dance Fever*. The film *12 Storeys* received good reviews at the Cannes Film Festival in France. Singapore also hosts the annual Singapore International Film

Esplanade—Theatres on the Bay

In October 2002, Singapore's newest and largest performing arts center opened: Esplanade—Theatres on the Bay. As its name says, this theater complex faces Marina Bay next to the park known as the Esplanade. Indoors, it can seat up to 4,270 people in four areas. Many more people can attend performances in its outdoor theater along the bay. The opening festival had three weeks of free concerts. The final concert was dedicated to Ong Teng Cheong, Singapore's first elected president and a professor of music. He helped plan the complex as a way for Singapore to become a global center for the arts.

Festival. Movies from 250 countries are shown in theaters throughout Singapore. Each year, Singaporeans see an average of about 3.5 movies in the nation's 131 movie theaters.

Sports for All, Sports for Life

Singaporeans young and old participate in sports. The warm climate makes outdoor activities possible year-round. Jogging, walking, and swimming are the three most popular sports for individuals. Walking and jogging paths wind through the parks and along the beaches and the reservoirs. Swimmers have the use of pools at twenty-eight swimming complexes. They also can swim in the country's coastal waters. Other water sports include sailing, wind surfing, water-skiing, and scuba diving. Tennis and golf are popular with some Singaporeans. Many Singaporeans work out at indoor and outdoor fitness centers.

The Changi Sailing Club sails by massive tankers in the harbor.

Mountain Men

On May 25, 1998, Edwin Siew and Khoo Swee Chiow became the first Singaporeans to reach the summit of Mount Everest in Tibet. Everest is the world's highest peak. The Singapore Mount Everest Expedition demonstrated Singapore's "can do" attitude. The climbing team failed in its first attempt to conquer Everest. In a second attempt, teamwork and determination brought them to the top. Siew and Khoo planted Singapore's flag on the top of the world. In 2002, Siew was featured in the National Day video "We Can Make It."

Singaporeans also enjoy watching sporting events. The British introduced horse racing at the Singapore Turf Club in 1843. Polo is another sport with horses. The Singapore Polo Club hosts polo matches. The first cricket game in Singapore was played at the Padang in 1852. The Singapore Cricket Club is still at the Padang. Cricket games are played there from March through September. During the rest of the year, the Padang becomes a rugby field. Singaporeans watch professional soccer games at National Stadium. Singapore has national badminton and table-tennis teams. They have placed well in the Southeast Asian Games and the Commonwealth Games.

Cricket has been played in Singapore since 1852.

Family, Food, Fun, and Festivals

SINGAPOREANS WORK HARD AND STUDY HARD, BUT THEY know how to have fun, too. They spend much time with their families and friends. Singaporeans are known for two of their favorite activities—eating and shopping. They have so many wonderful foods to choose from, and the number of stores and shops continues to grow. Singaporeans have special fun during their many ethnic and national festivals held throughout the year. At the festivals, they eat special foods, wear traditional clothing, and listen to traditional music.

Opposite: **Family time in Singapore**

Shopping is a favorite pastime in Singapore.

At home in Singapore

Singaporeans at Home

Whether they're flats or single-family houses, Singaporean homes are clean and comfortable. In the housing estates, some families have two flats next to each other. Grandparents live in one flat. Grown children with their own children live in the other one. In this way, grandparents can baby-sit the grandchildren while their parents are at work. It also makes it easier for grown children to take care of their aging parents. Most Singaporeans live at home with their families until they get married. However, some single Singaporeans have started moving out on their own.

Flats in the housing estates have become expensive to own. However, Singaporeans sign up and wait for the chance to purchase their first flat or to buy a larger one. Families living in housing estates have their own parks, schools, libraries, and community centers. They also can shop, buy food in the markets, eat out in areas called hawker centers, and do their banking without leaving the estates. Some residents even work in small factories or service industries in the estates.

Singaporean families don't spend all their time at their housing estate, however. They visit the Zoological Gardens, the Botanic Gardens, Singapore's museums or nature reserves, or Sentosa Island for a day of fun. Most families travel around Singapore on buses or the MRT trains. Few families have cars, because they are so expensive. When Singaporeans take longer vacations, they sometimes go to Malaysia or other parts of Southeast Asia.

Buying a Car

To control traffic congestion and air pollution, the government limits car ownership. To buy a car, Singaporeans first must obtain a special certificate that costs about U.S.$30,000. Only 4,000 certificates are available per month. To complete the purchase of a car, the new owner must also pay a 45 percent import fee and a 150 percent registration tax. The final cost for a compact car is about U.S.$60,000. To keep the car running, the driver must pay a high fuel tax for gasoline. Besides, every year the lucky car owner pays a road tax based on the size of the car's engine. The government's system must be working. Only 30 percent of Singaporean households have cars. Singaporeans rely on public transportation to get around their island.

Each of Singapore's ethnic groups prepares its own kind of delicious food. Malay, Indian, and some kinds of Chinese foods are hot and spicy. However, rice is common to all of these cuisines. Besides foods from the main ethnic groups, restaurants in Singapore serve foods from many other countries, such as Japan, the United States, and France.

Singapore's Chinese have several of their own cuisines because the early Chinese came from different provinces in China. However, each Chinese meal is supposed to have sweet, bitter, acidic, salty, and spicy tastes. In that way, yin and yang are in balance. Typical Cantonese dishes are fish steamed with soy sauce, won ton soup, and suckling pig. Hokkien cuisine features spring rolls and lots of noodles. Sweet potatoes, dried shrimp, and *yong tau foo*, deep-fried bean curd, are Hakka specialities. *Dim sum* is a type of Chinese lunch. It's made up of a variety of small dumplings, egg rolls, and other cooked doughs that are stuffed with vegetables, pork, beef, or shrimp.

This woman prepares Peranakan food.

The Peranakans, who are part Chinese and part Malay, have their own special dishes. The most popular one is *poh piah*, a spring roll stuffed with turnips, bamboo shoots, bean curd, shrimp, and pork. The best-known Malay dish is *satay*. Small pieces of beef, chicken, or lamb are

Hawker Centers

Most Singaporeans eat out at least twice a week. Their favorite spots are the hawker centers. At one time, vendors sold, or "hawked," food on Singapore's streets. The government moved them into covered outdoor centers, called hawker centers. In each center, Chinese, Malay, and Indian vendors have stalls where they specialize in one or two dishes. There are also a few indoor, air-conditioned hawker centers. At the centers, customers find a table and select food from various vendors. Government inspectors check each stall, give it a grade of A through D for its level of cleanliness, and post the grade for customers to see. A full meal at a hawker center costs about U.S.$3.

skewered and grilled. They are dipped in peanut sauce and served with rice wrapped in coconut-palm leaves, cucumbers, and onions. One of the most famous Indian dishes is chicken *tandoori*. Chicken soaked in lime, yogurt, and spices is cooked slowly in a clay oven called a *tandoor*. Because many Hindu Indians are vegetarians, their dishes include a wide variety of vegetables and, of course, rice.

Clothing in Singapore

Today, most Singaporeans wear Western-style clothes at work and at home. Some more-traditional Singaporeans wear clothing from their ethnic group on weekends or on vacation. Most others save traditional clothing for festivals and weddings.

The sarong has become a symbol of the Malay. This a long, loose-fitting cloth that is folded and tucked around the waist to hang like a skirt. Both Malay men and women wear sarongs. Above the sarong, women wear a tight-fitting blouse called a *kebaya* or a loose-fitting blouse called a *baju kurung*. Men wear a loose-fitting shirt called a *baju*. For formal occasions, the men wear loose slacks. As Muslims, both men and women wear headgear. A woman's headdress is called a *telekung*; a man's is called a *songkok*.

A woman wearing a sari visits Mariamman Temple.

During Chinese New Year, some Chinese women wear a tight-fitting dress called a *cheongsam*. It has a high, stiff collar and side slits that allow for sitting and walking. Peranakan women used to wear sarongs and kebayas. Now very few wear this clothing. Chinese and Peranakan men wear Western clothing.

Indian women wear their saris to temple and for festivals. Many women also wear them at home. A sari is a long piece of cotton or silk cloth. The material is draped around the body and over one shoulder. Indian women also wear a tight-fitting blouse called a *choli* with the sari. Indian men sometimes wear a colored *lungi* or a white *mundi*. Both of these garments are similar to a sarong.

A basket shop on
Arab Street

Stalls and Malls

Singaporeans are known for their love of shopping. They can
shop until they drop from the end of May through July. During
that time, Singaporeans and tourists take part in the Great
Singapore Sale. Major department stores and shops throughout the island offer large discounts on their goods. One famous
department store is the Yue Hwa Chinese Products Store. The
goods in this store range from silk clothing to medicines—all
from China. Small shops and stalls on Arab Street sell baskets,
mats, and textiles. Outdoor markets along the Singapore
River have second-hand clothing, handmade jewelry, and
woodcarvings.

Raffles City Shopping Centre offers luxury goods for its shoppers.

Singapore's famous shopping malls are located in Orchard Road, Suntec City, and Marina Square. Singaporeans can purchase luxurious goods in stores such as Cartier, Bulgari, and Tiffany. Many other well-known U.S. and European chains have shops in Singapore's upscale malls. Funan Centre is a mall that sells only computers. Singaporeans can buy just about any brand of computer there. Sim Lim Square has audio and video equipment, electronic games, and computer software.

Festivals and Holidays

Singapore's festivals and holidays provide food, entertainment, and fun throughout the year. In the early fall, Singapore's Chinese community celebrates the Moon Cake Festival, also called the Lantern Festival. Round moon cakes are sold in shops. Children carry colorful paper lanterns that come in all shapes and sizes. Some are as large as dragons. A contest for the best lantern is held at the Chinese Gardens.

In the early winter, Hindus from southern India hold the four-day Thanksgiving festival called *pong gal*. They cook rice in a new pot and let it boil over as a sign of prosperity. Later, the Chinese celebrate Chinese New Year for fifteen days with parades, special foods, and fireworks. The Chingay Parade, held during Chinese New Year, is multicultural, for all of Singapore's ethnic people. Floats, dancers, and skateboarders are all part of the parade.

Chinese Chess

Chinese chess is played by Singaporeans young and old, male and female. The chessboard has sixty-four squares, just like a Western chessboard. However, the pieces are placed where the lines cross instead of within the squares. The object is to capture the opponent's pieces.

In April, Singapore has its Food Festival. Vendors in hawker centers and chefs in upscale restaurants tempt customers with special dishes. The Dragon Boat Festival takes place in June at East Coast Park. Longboats with about twenty paddlers each take part in races.

The big festival of the summer is National Day, on August 9. Singaporeans celebrate their nation's independence with a huge parade, speeches, and fireworks. At the same time, they are also celebrating the economic miracle that they—as united Singaporeans—have achieved in such a short time.

Multicultural dancers perform at the Chinese New Year Chingay Parade.

National Holidays in Singapore

New Year's Day	January 1
Chinese New Year	January or February
Hari Raya Haji	February
Good Friday	March or April
Labor Day	May 1
Vesak Day	May
National Day	August 9
Deepavali	October or November
Christmas	December 25
Hari Raya Puasa	December or January

Timeline

Singapore's History

People are living in what is now Singapore.   A.D. 100s

Malay people are living in a settlement called   1200s
Temasek on Singapore.

Sultan Iskandar Shah, or Parameswara,   1389–1391
rules Singapore.

Empires of Java and Siam attack Singapore;   Late 1300s
the sultan flees and sets up Sultanate of
Malacca on Malay Peninsula.

Singapore becomes part of the Sultanate   Late 1390s
of Malacca.

Portuguese overcome the sultanate.   1511

The Dutch gain control of Malacca.   1641

Thomas Stamford Raffles selects Singapore for   1819
an East India Company trading post.

Britain acquires Singapore and   1824
surrounding islands.

Singapore becomes part of the Straits   1826
Settlements.

World History

2500 B.C.   Egyptians build the Pyramids
and the Sphinx in Giza.

563 B.C.   The Buddha is born in India.

A.D. 313   The Roman emperor Constantine
recognizes Christianity.

610   The Prophet Muhammad begins preaching
a new religion called Islam.

1054   The Eastern (Orthodox) and Western
(Roman) Churches break apart.

1066   William the Conqueror defeats
the English in the Battle of Hastings.

1095   Pope Urban II proclaims the First Crusade.

1215   King John seals the Magna Carta.

1300s   The Renaissance begins in Italy.

1347   The Black Death sweeps through Europe.

1453   Ottoman Turks capture Constantinople,
conquering the Byzantine Empire.

1492   Columbus arrives in North America.

1500s   The Reformation leads to the birth
of Protestantism.

1776   The Declaration of Independence
is signed.

1789   The French Revolution begins.

Singapore's History

Singapore becomes capital of the Straits Settlements.	1832
The Straits Settlements become a crown colony of Britain.	1867
Singapore is one of the world's greatest ports.	1930s
Singapore falls to Japanese forces during World War II.	1942
Japanese surrender to British at the end of World War II.	1945
Singapore becomes a separate crown colony.	1946
Singapore holds elections for a legislative council; Lee Kuan Yew helps found the People's Action Party (PAP).	1954
Britain grants Singapore internal self-government.	1958
Elections are held; Lee Kuan Yew becomes Singapore's first prime minister.	1959
Singapore becomes part of the Federation of Malaysia.	1963
Singapore becomes an independent republic with Lee Kuan Yew as prime minister and joins the United Nations (UN).	1965
Singapore helps found the Association of Southeast Asian Nations (ASEAN).	1967
Britain withdraws last military forces from Singapore.	1971
Goh Chok Tong becomes Singapore's second prime minister.	1990
Singapore holds it first presidential election and elects Ong Teng Cheong.	1993
S. R. Nathan is elected president.	1999
Prime Minister Goh starts the Speak Good English Movement.	2000

World History

1865	The American Civil War ends.
1914	World War I breaks out.
1917	The Bolshevik Revolution brings communism to Russia.
1929	Worldwide economic depression begins.
1939	World War II begins, following the German invasion of Poland.
1945	World War II ends.
1957	The Vietnam War starts.
1969	Humans land on the moon.
1975	The Vietnam War ends.
1979	Soviet Union invades Afghanistan.
1983	Drought and famine in Africa.
1989	The Berlin Wall is torn down, as communism crumbles in Eastern Europe.
1991	Soviet Union breaks into separate states.
1992	Bill Clinton is elected U.S. president.
2000	George W. Bush is elected U.S. president.
2001	Terrorists attack World Trade Towers, New York and the Pentagon, Washington, D.C.

Fast Facts

Official name:	Republic of Singapore
Capital:	Singapore
Official languages:	Mandarin, English, Malay, Tamil

Downtown Singapore

Singapore's flag

A view from Bukit Timah

Official religion:	None
Year of founding:	1965
National anthem:	*"Majulah Singapura"* ("Onward Singapore")
Government:	Multiparty, parliamentary republic
Chief of state:	President
Head of government:	Prime minister
Area and dimensions:	255 square miles (660 sq km) Greatest distance north to south: 14 miles (23 km) Greatest distance east to west: 26 miles (42 km)
Latitude and longitude of geographic center:	1° 22' North, 103° 48' East
Water borders:	Johor Strait to the north, between Singapore and Malaysia; Singapore Strait to the southeast and the Strait of Malacca to the southwest, both between Singapore and Indonesia
Highest elevation:	Bukit Timah, 581 feet (177 m) above sea level
Lowest elevation:	Sea level, along the coast
Average temperature extremes:	In January, 79°F (26°C); in July, 81°F (27°C)
Average precipitation extremes:	About 7 inches (18 cm) a month, May to September; more than 10 inches (25 cm) a month, November to March
National population (2001 census):	4,131,200

The Botanic Gardens

Currency

Population of largest housing estates (2002 est):		
Tampines		217,900
Jurong		205,400
Bedok		199,800
Woodlands		192,700
Hougang		165,900

Famous landmarks:

▶ *Bukit Timah Nature Reserve*, west central

▶ *Fort Canning Hill and Park*, City Center

▶ *Jurong Bird Park*, southwest

▶ *The Padang*, City Center

▶ *Raffles Hotel*, City Center

▶ *Sentosa Island*, south

▶ *Singapore Botanic Gardens*, south central

▶ *Singapore Zoological Gardens*, north central

▶ *Sri Mariamman Temple*, Chinatown

▶ *Sultan Mosque*, Arab District

▶ *Thian Hock Keng Temple*, Chinatown

Industry: Manufacturing makes up about 22 percent of Singapore's economy. The main manufactured goods include refined oil, electronics equipment such as computer goods and chips, textiles, transportation equipment, and ships. Import and export trade remains a key part of Singapore's economy, with Singapore as the world's busiest port. Financial services such as banks, insurance companies, and a stock exchange make Singapore an international financial center.

Currency: The Singapore dollar (S$); in March 2003, U.S.$1 = S$1.75

System of weights and measures: Metric system

Young Singaporean students

Literacy rate (2000):	93 percent

Common Malay words and phrases:		
	Apa khabar? (apa khabar)	Hello/How are you?
	Bagaimana saya pergi ke...? (ba-gai-ma-na sa-ya per-gee-ke)	How do I get to . . .?
	Harganya berapa? (HAR-ganya ber A-pa)	How much does it cost?
	Maafkan saya. (ma-fkan sa-ya)	Excuse me.
	Sila (SEE-la)	Please
	Selamat jalan. (Se-LA-mat JA-lan)	Good-bye.
	Terima kasih. (TREE-ma KA-see)	Thank you.
	Tidak (TEE-dak)	No
	Tolong! (TO-long)	Help!
	Ya (ya)	Yes

Famous Singaporeans:		
	Gopal Baratham *Novelist*	(?–2002)
	Georgette Chen *Artist*	(1906–1993)
	Sultan Hussein *Malay ruler of Singapore*	(early 1800s)
	Agnes Joaquim *Discovered orchid (1893) that became national flower*	(late 1800s–1900s)
	Lee Kuan Yew *Politician, first prime minister (1959–1990)*	(1923–)
	Catherine Lim *Novelist, short story writer*	(1943–)
	Edwin Siew *Mountain climber*	(1971–)
	Thomas Stamford Raffles *Trader, founder of Singapore*	(1781–1826)

Lee Kuan Yew

To Find Out More

Books

▶ Layton, Lesley, and Pang Guek Cheng. *Singapore*. Cultures of the World. Tarrytown, N.Y.: Marshall Cavendish, 2002.

▶ Liu, Gretchen. *Singapore: A Pictorial History, 1819–2000*. Singapore: Archipelago Press, 2001.

▶ Perera, Audrey. *The Simple Guide to Customs and Etiquette in Singapore*. Kent, England: Global Books, 1996.

▶ Thomas, Matt. *Singapore: Faces and Places*. Chanhassen, Minn.: Child's World, 2002.

▶ Warren, William. *Singapore: City of Gardens*. Singapore: Periplus Editions, 2000.

▶ Wee, Jessie. *Singapore*. Major World Nations. Philadelphia: Chelsea House, 2000.

▶ Wibisono, Djoko; David Wong; and Luca Invernizzi. *The Food of Singapore: Authentic Recipes from the Manhattan of the East*. Singapore: Periplus, 2001.

▶ Wright, David. *Singapore*. Children of the World. Milwaukee: Gareth Stevens Children's Books, 1991.

Videos

▶ *Singapore*. Fodor. Fort Worth, Texas: TravelWorld Video, 1989. A 45-minute tour of the sights and sounds of Singapore; includes a booklet with facts about the country.

▶ *Singapore*. Rand McNally and Company. San Ramon, Calif.: International Video Network, 1995. A 30-minute videocassette highlighting Singapore's growth from a small island kingdom to a world economic power.

Web Sites

▶ **Authoritative Singaporean History Site: Knowledgenet Singapore**
http://www.knowledgenet.com.sg
Includes pages with biographies, oral histories, and timelines, as well as the Student Café, with history pages designed by Singaporean students.

▶ **Singapore Infomap: The National Web Site**
http://www.sg
Everything from arts to travel, Facts at a Glance, background on current events and exhibits, and insights on what it is like to live and work in Singapore.

▶ **Singapore Republic**
http://www.singaporerepublic.com
A daily news web site with updates on Singapore's government, economy, sports, and other aspects of Singaporean life, with useful links.

▶ **Singapore Zoological Gardens**
http://www.zoo.com.sg
Includes pages on the zoo's history, visits to its natural habitats, and links to Singapore's Night Safari and Jurong Bird Park.

▶ **Sing Singapore 2002**
http://www.singsingapore.org.sg
Features songs written by Singaporeans for Singaporeans, including songs for National Day celebrations.

Organizations and Embassies

▶ **Embassy of the Republic of Singapore**
3501 International Place, NW
Washington, DC 20008
(202) 537-3100

▶ **Singapore Tourism Board**
Two Prudential Plaza
180 North Stetson Avenue
Suite 2615
Chicago, IL 60601
(312) 938-1888

Index

Page numbers in *italics* indicate illustrations.

Meet the Author

PATRICIA K. KUMMER writes and edits textbook materials and nonfiction books for children and young adults from her home office in Lisle, Illinois. She earned a Bachelor of Arts degree in history from the College of St. Catherine in St. Paul, Minnesota, and a Master of Arts degree in history from Marquette University in Milwaukee, Wisconsin. Before starting her career in publishing, she taught social studies at the junior-high/middle-school level.

Since then, she has written about American, African, Asian, and European history for textbook publishers and "A Guide to Writing and Speaking" in World Book's *Word Power Library*. More recently she wrote *Côte d'Ivoire*, *Ukraine*, and *Tibet* in the Children's Press series Enchantment of the World and thirty books about the U.S. states. One of her favorite projects was writing a commissioned biography for Jerry Reinsdorf, chairman of the Chicago Bulls and the Chicago White Sox. The biography commemorates the life of his administrative assistant, who died leaving a three-year-old daughter. The book was based totally on interviews. It will be presented to the daughter when she is about thirteen years old.

"Writing books about people, states, and countries requires a great deal of research," she says. "To me, researching is the most fun part of a project. My research begins by going online. For this book, I found several good Web sites, many of them from departments of Singapore's government. Then, I compiled a list of the most recent books on Singapore. From there, I went to the library. For the books my library didn't have, I placed interlibrary loan requests. To keep up with events in Singapore, I signed onto a list-serv that sent me daily news reports on Singapore.

"When I needed answers that I could not find in any of these sources, I e-mailed questions to the Singapore Tourism Board in Singapore, the Housing Development Board, and the Singapore Mint. Overnight or within a few days, I received answers from staff at the various boards."

Ms. Kummer hopes that this book will help young people better understand how the nation of Singapore came to be and how its multicultural people have worked hard to gain a leading position in the family of nations.

Photo Credits